GREEK PROTHETIC VOWEL

PHILOLOGICAL MONOGRAPHS
OF THE
AMERICAN PHILOLOGICAL ASSOCIATION

NUMBER 31

Edited by
JOHN J. KEANEY
Princeton University

Legati Hahniani ope
hic liber prodit

Accepted for publication by the Committee on the Publication of Monographs
of The American Philological Association

THE GREEK PROTHETIC VOWEL

By
WILLIAM F. WYATT, JR.
Brown University

Published for
THE AMERICAN PHILOLOGICAL ASSOCIATION

By the Press of
CASE WESTERN RESERVE UNIVERSITY
1972

Library of Congress Catalogue Number: 73-171069
ISBN 0-8295-0218-1

Printed in the United States of America

PREFACE

My work on the Greek Prothetic Vowel represents the latest
— and I hope final — stage in a series of works which I have
directed against the laryngeal theory of Indo-European phonology. That theory holds that certain consonants, lost in all Indo-
European languages save sometimes Hittite, were responsible,
both for the color of a vowel (a e o = H_1e H_2e H_3e) and for its
length (ā ē ō = eH_1 eH_2 eH_3), and also, between consonants, for
the vowel *schwa* (ə = CHC). As a graduate student I was
convinced by Professor Joshua Whatmough of the correctness of
this theory, and indeed set out, under his direction, to demon-
strate the effects of laryngeal consonants on Homeric scansion. I
soon realized that laryngeals had nothing to do with Homer
(*Metrical Lengthening in Homer*, Rome, 1969), and that a purely
Homeric answer to Homeric problems was required: I did not,
though, yet doubt the existence of laryngeals in Proto-Indo-
European. Later, while preparing a course in Indo-European
phonology at the University of Washington and investigating the
theoretical foundations of the laryngeal theory, I found that such
foundations were few and weak ("Structural Linguistics and the
Laryngeal Theory", *Language* 40[1964]138-52). Hence the laryngeal theory, in my thinking at least, had to be replaced, and
in 1970 (*Indo-European /a/*, Philadelphia), I published my
identification of Proto-Indo-European [a] and [ə], thus removing
from the Proto-Indo-European phonetic inventory a vocalizable
laryngeal consonant. Difficulties remained, though, for as Professor Werner Winter had pointed out to me already in 1966, [a]
and [ə] seemed to contrast initially in cases of so-called Greek
prothesis, [a] remaining in Greek and Sanskrit, [ə] remaining only
in Greek. My first answer to his observation appears on pages 24-
26 of *Indo-European /a/*; my final answer appears in the pages

which follow. Whether or not my views of Proto-Indo-European laryngeals are accepted, I do hope that my work will have shown that laryngeals are not a cure-all, and that by positing them where they do not belong, scholars have frequently frustrated a true, or at least a better, explanation. In short, I hope that something positive will have resulted.

In my work I have been helped by discussions with linguists at Brown and Ohio State, to the latter of whom I owe the observation — which I here pass on — that the environments specified in rule 6) of page 119 do not form any sort of natural class and hence cannot be literally correct: they are an approximation only, and are more suitable for a computer program than for a natural language. There does in fact exist a prothesis-creating computer program prepared by Gerald M. Rubin, programmer extraordinary for Brown University's Linguistics Department, which has been of great help and which has saved me from numerous errors.

I also wish to thank several members of the American Philological Association: J. Arthur Hanson, former editor of the Association's *Transactions*, who, in denying me the pages of *TAPA*, encouraged me to expand an article into a monograph; John J. Keaney, current editor of *TAPA*, for preparing a difficult manuscript for the printer; David W. Packard, who provided the computer program which produced the printed version of this work; and John J. Bateman, who oversaw the whole.

Providence, 7 August 1970

TABLE OF CONTENTS

ABBREVIATIONS

(Classical authors are abbreviated as in LSJ)

Frisk = H. Frisk, *Griechisches etymologisches Wörterbuch*, 2 vols., Heidelberg, 1960-70

GEW = Frisk

HSCP = Harvard Studies in Classical Philology

IG = Inscriptiones graecae

KEW = Mayrhofer

KZ = Zeitschrift für vergleichende Sprachforschung

Leaf = W. Leaf (Ed.), The Iliad, 2 vols. 2nd Ed., London 1900-1902 (Reprinted Amsterdam, 1960)

LSJ = Liddell-Scott-Jones, *A Greek-English Lexicon*, 9th Ed. Oxford, 1940

Mayrhofer = M. Mayrhofer, *Kurzgefasstes etymologisches Wörterbuch des Altindischen*, 3 vols., Heidelberg 1953-

PLF = E. Lobel and D.L. Page, *Poetarum lesbiorum fragmenta*, Oxford, 1955

Pok. = J. Pokorny, *Indogermanisches etymologisches Wörterbuch*, Bern, 1959

Walde-Hofmann = A. Walde, *Lateinisches etymologisches Wörterbuch*, 3rd Ed. Revised by J.B. Hofmann, 2 vols., Heidelberg 1938-1954

BIBLIOGRAPHY

Antilla 1969: R. Antilla, *Proto-Indo-European Schwebeablaut* (University of California Publications: Linguistics 58), Berkeley and Los Angeles, 1969

Austin 1941: W.M. Austin, "The prothetic vowel in Greek", *Language* 17:83-92

Beekes 1969: R.S.P. Beekes, *The Development of the Proto-Indo-European Laryngeals in Greek* (Janua Linguarum Series Practica 38), The Hague, 1969

Beveniste 1935: E. Benveniste, *Origines de la formation des noms en indo-européen*, Paris, 1935

Carpenter 1946: R. Carpenter, *Folk Tale, Fiction, and Saga in the Homeric Epics*, Berkeley, 1946

Chadwick 1963: J. Chadwick & L. Baumbach, "The Mycenaean Greek Vocabulary", Glotta 41: 147-271

Chantraine, P.: 1933: *La formation des noms en grec ancien*, Paris, 1933

―― 1948: *Grammaire homérique*, Vol. 1, 2nd Ed., Paris, 1948

―― 1968: *Dictionnaire étymologique de la langue grecque*, Vol. I, Paris, 1968

Cowgill 1965: W. Cowgill, "Evidence in Greek", in Winter 1965b: 142-180

Crossland 1958: R. Crossland, "Remarks on the Indo-European Laryngeals", *Archivum Linguisticum* 10:79-99

Cuny 1943: A. Cuny, *Recherches sur le vocalisme, le consonantisme et la formation des racines en nostratique*, Paris, 1943

Debrunner 1907: A. Debrunner, "Zu den konsonantischen *io-*Präsentien im Griechischen", *Indogermanische Forschungen* 21:201-276

Edgerton 1943: F. Edgerton, "The Indo-european semivowels", *Language* 19:83-124

Hamp 1960: E.P. Hamp, "Notes on Early Greek Phonology", *Glotta* 38:187-203

Kiparsky 1968: P. Kiparsky, "Sonorant Clusters in Greek", *Language* (1967) 43:619-635 (appeared 1968)

Kühner-Blass 1890: R. Kühner, *Ausführliche Grammatik der griechischen Sprache* 1. Teil, 2 vols., 3rd ed. rev. by F. Blass

Kuryłowicz 1956: J. Kuryłowicz, *Apophonie en indo-européen*, Wrocław, 1956

Lejeune, M. 1943: "Sur les traitements grecs des sonantes", *Revue des études anciennes* 44: 131-149

—— 1955: *Traité de phonétique grecque*, 2nd ed., Paris, 1955

Leumann 1950: M. Leumann, *Homerische Wörter* (Schweizerische Beiträge zur Altertumswissenschaft 3), Basel, 1950

Meyer 1896: G. Meyer, *Griechische Grammatik*, 3rd Ed., Leipzig, 1896

Nagy 1970: G. Nagy, *Greek Dialects and the Transformation of an Indo-European Process*, Cambridge (Mass.), 1970

Nikitina 1962: F. Nikitina, "Protetičeskije glasnyje drevne-grečeskogo jazyka kak refleksy indojevropejskix ščelevyx", *Voprosy jazykoznanija* 1962.1.81-86

Polomé 1965: E. Polomé, "The Laryngeal Theory so far: a critical bibliographical survey" in Winter 1965b:9-78

Puhvel 1960: J. Puhvel, *Laryngeals and the Indo-European Verb* (University of California Publications: Linguistics 21), Berkeley and Los Angeles, 1960

Schmidt 1893: J. Schmidt, "Assimilationen benachbarten einander nicht berührender vokale im griechischen" *KZ* 32:321-394

Schulze 1966: W. Schulze, *Kleine Schriften*, 2nd Ed., Göttingen, 1966

Schwyzer, E. 1923: *Dialectorum graecarum exempla epigraphica potiora,* Leipzig 1923 (reprinted Hildesheim, 1960)

—— 1939: *Griechische Grammatik*, Vol. 1, Munich, 1939

Seiler 1950: H.-J. Seiler, *Die Primären griechischen Steigerungs-formen,* Hamburg, 1950

—— 1957: "Zum prothetischen Vokal im Griechischen: Ablaut-ende Präposition: *en/n̥*", *KZ* 75:1-23

Solmsen 1901: F. Solmsen, *Untersuchungen zur griechischen Laut und Verslehre*, Strassburg, 1901

Sommer 1905: F. Sommer, *Griechische Lautstudien*, Strassburg, 1905

Strömberg 1944: R. Strömberg, *Griechische Wortstudien*, Göteborg, 1944

Szemerényi, O. 1960: *Studies in the Indo-European System of Numerals*, Heidelberg, 1960

—— 1964: *Syncope in Greek and Indo-European and the Nature of the Indo-European Accent* (Istituto Universitario Orientale di Napoli, Quaderni della Sezione linguistica degli annali 3), Naples, 1964

Winter, W. 1950: *Studien über "prothetische Vokal" im Griechischen*, Hamburg, 1950

—— 1952: "An Indo-European Prefix *n̥ 'Together with'", *Language* 28:186-191

—— 1965a: "Tocharian Evidence" in Winter 1965b:190-211

—— 1965b: *Evidence for Laryngeals*, W. Winter ed., The Hague, 1965

Wyatt, W. 1964: "Structural Linguistics and the Laryngeal Theory", *Language* 40:138-152

—— 1969: "Greek Names in -σσος/-ττος," *Glotta* 46:6-14 (1968: appeared 1969)

—— 1969a: "Early Greek /y/", *Glotta* 46:229-237 (1968: appeared 1969)

—— 1969b: *Metrical Lengthening in Homer* (Incunabula Graeca 35), Rome, 1969

—— 1970: *Indo-European /a/* (Haney Foundation Series 7), Philadelphia, 1970

THE PROBLEM

1.0 There is no general agreement today concerning the origins of the Greek "prothetic vowel".[1] Nor is this surprising, for there is no agreement on whether prothesis is a phenomenon inherited from Proto-Indo-European, either a full vowel or a vocalized laryngeal; or whether these sounds arose after the PIE period as the result of anticipation of voicing in a following resonant, either in Greek alone, or in Greek together with Armenian. What is perhaps a little surprising, though, is the complacency with which this uncertainty has been accepted, for, taken literally, a prothetic vowel of sporadic appearance constitutes a threat to the doctrine that phonological processes operate in a regular fashion and allow of no exceptions unless interfered with by morphological considerations. Perhaps scholars have felt that there is a phonological explanation, but that it has not yet been discovered. In what follows I shall approach the problem anew in hopes of providing an account which will prove that the development is regular and principled.

First we must define and delimit the problem. A prothetic vowel is assumed in Greek when a Greek word has an initial vowel in a word of Indo-European origin whose cognates in all other IE languages (except sometimes Armenian) show an initial consonant, and only then: thus Grk. ὄνομα beside Lat. *nōmen*, Skt. *nāma* 'name' contains a prothetic vowel, whereas Grk. ἠώς < *ausōs* beside Lat. *aurōra* Skt. *uṣáḥ* 'dawn' does not, even though the Skt. word lacks the initial /a/.[2] I shall be concerned

---

[1] For general discussions of prothesis cf. Lejeune 1955:127-129, 148, 181-182, 273 and Schwyzer 1939:412-413; and for bibliography on the problem: Schwyzer loc. cit. and Szemerényi 1964:7 fn. 1.

[2] Initial unaccented IE */a/ disappears in Skt., cf. Wyatt 1970:26-28. For the Greek developments, cf. Kiparsky 1968, who demonstrates that it is unnecessary to posit IE */a:/ in this word.

here only with those prothetic vowels which appear before the resonant consonants and semivowels (/r l m n y w/), and hence shall not consider cases of prothesis before /st/- (ἀστεροπή beside στεροπή 'lightning'; ἀστήρ beside Lat. *stella* 'star') or /kʰtʰ/- (ἐχθές beside χθές 'yesterday'; ἰχθύς beside Arm. *ǰukn* 'fish'). These are important matters, equally deserve the name of prothesis, and the mechanism of prothesis in both cases could conceivably in part be the same, but it seems legitimate to separate off the resonants as a group. But even within the resonants there are restrictions and limitations. Prothesis is the rule before IE */r/-[3] and never occurs before IE */y/-, though a partly analogous development takes place there:[4] neither of these consonants need concern us, at least at the outset. As a result the problematic cases of prothesis are those that appear before /l m n w/.[5]

The reason, or one of the reasons, that a satisfactory explanation for prothesis has not yet been found is that the occurrence of prothesis is sporadic and inconsistent within Greek: sporadic in that not all Grk. words beginning with /l m n w/ show prothesis (cf. ἐλεύθερος 'free' beside λέγω 'I say'); inconsistent in that the same root may show forms both with and without prothesis (ἀλείφω 'anoint with oil' beside λίπος 'fat'), and indeed one and the same word may appear now with and now without prothesis (ἐέλδομαι beside ἔλδομαι 'wish, long for', both from *weldomai*.) The sporadic occurrence of prothesis renders difficult a purely phonological explanation, for the same sound should behave always in the same way, while its inconsistency within single morphemes seems to exclude any other kind of explanation, though some sort of phonotactic explanation might serve, as we shall see.

---

[3] Or so it is usually assumed. Cf. below 6.2.

[4] I refer to the two-fold development of */y/-, for */y/- develops sometimes to /h/ and sometimes to /dz/ under conditions explained in Wyatt 1969a and 6.5 below.

[5] Another problem connected with prothesis is the color of the prothetic vowel, a problem which, though logically secondary, has to many seemed to provide the fatal obstacle to any explanation, and a problem which will be treated, though perhaps not solved, in 6.6.7 below.

1.1 I have tried to imagine all the various ways that prothesis might be explained and the objections which could be raised to these explanations. Explanations fall first into two types on the lines of the presumed date of origin: some feel that prothesis is an inherited phenomenon, others that it is an innovation. Both of these explanations can be further subdivided into three groups: those that regard the mechanism of prothesis as being due to phonological, phonotactic, or morphological factors. It may be that not all of these possible positions have actually been adopted, and some scholars may have admitted different origins for individual cases. The lines are in any event apt to be blurred between the explanations, but it has seemed best to discuss them all individually as separate and discrete theories.

1.1.1 Those scholars who hold that prothesis is a phenomenon inherited from PIE tend to identify the prothetic vowel with one or more of the PIE laryngeal consonants.[6] Thus Benveniste (1935:152) was able to explain the "prothesis" in Grk. ἀλέξω 'ward off' (3.1.2 below) as opposed to Skt. rakṣati 'protects' in terms of his theories of IE root structure: ἀλκή 'strength' derives from *a_2el-k-, his form I of the root, while ἀλέξω and rakṣati come from *a_2lek-, his form II of the root, with both */a_2e/ and */a_2/ developing to /a/ in Grk. and /a_2/ disappearing in Skt. Austin (1941: 83-92), who does not restrict the occurrence of prothesis to position before a resonant, took the notion of laryngeal origin of prothesis further still, and sought to explain nearly all cases of prothesis by means of laryngeals. He states as his rule (1941:85): "In Indo-Hittite bases beginning with the first, third, or fourth laryngeal the first syllable was retained everywhere if it was in the full grade. If the first syllable was in the reduced grade, it was lost everywhere except in Hittite, where it appears as a- or ha-, Greek, where it appears as ἀ-, ἐ-, or ὀ-, and Armenian, where

---

[6] The clearest exposition of laryngeal theory known to me is Lejeune's (1955:173-176). For a history with bibliography of the development of laryngeal theory cf. Polomé 1965, and for a very useful bibliography (all but complete to 1950), Puhvel 1960:1-13.

it appears as *a-*, (*e/i-*)." This rule accounts for the majority of certain cases of prothesis, as well as a number of others, but turns out to be unsatisfactory because it requires too many ad hoc IE reconstructions, and, more importantly, because it fails in spite of Austin's efforts (1941:88-91) to account for Greek words in which prothesis alternates either with aspiration or with smooth breathing (ἐέλδομαι ~ ἔλδομαι, ἐέρση ~ ἔρση). A sound under the same phonetic conditions should either always remain or always disappear.

More recently, scholars have tended to back away from Austin's extreme position and to assume laryngeal origin only where independent evidence for a laryngeal exists. Nikitina (1962: 81-86) ascribes prothesis to laryngeals only in cases like ἄησι 'blows' which have cognates in Hittite containing initial ḫ, as in ḫwantes 'winds'; or where long sonants occur in Homer (ἀείρω 'lift' beside ἀποέρση 'sweep away'); or in morphemes which also display Attic reduplication. Cowgill (1965:151-153) is similarly cautious, and even excludes ὄνομα (generally assumed to derive from *$H_3nom\underset{o}{n}$) from the constellation of forms with earlier laryngeal because of the absence of ḫ- or a- in Hitt. *laman*. It is his view that initial laryngeal before resonant (/HR/) is always vocalized in Grk., and that therefore εἴκοσι versus ἴκατι 'twenty' (< *wīkmti) and ἔρση versus ἐέρση 'dew' (< *wersā) do not contain prothesis of laryngeal origin. By doing so he avoids the difficulty inevitably faced by Austin and others, that in one and the same morpheme a phoneme should always appear in the same phonetic shape, a difficulty seen in ἀλείφω : λίπος, and a difficulty which invalidates the view that all prothetic vowels develop from earlier laryngeals. But of course there must have been laryngeals for the prothetic vowel to have developed from, and as I have endeavored to show elsewhere (Wyatt 1964, 1970), there is very good evidence that there were no such things as laryngeal consonants in IE with the properties assigned them by laryngealists. The Hitt. evidence in this case, though indeed at least superficially impressive, in fact can be used to elucidate prothesis only before */w/-, and does not explain all cases even there. Hence the laryngeal theory cannot be taken as a serious explanation for prothesis in Greek.[7]

Other scholars, while accepting that prothesis is in some cases at least of laryngeal origin, have felt that it came about as a more literally prothetic vowel. R. A. Crossland (1958:83-87) has developed the view that prothesis arose before */hw/- of whatever origin. Thus he accepts that ἄησι derives from earlier *hwēti (< IE *Hwēti), but also feels that ἀείρω 'raise' is to be connected with Lith. svéŕti 'to weigh', and therefore shows prothesis before */hw/- < IE */sw/-. Crossland's attempt is the more admirable for the fact that he does not regard prothesis as the vocalization of a laryngeal, but rather as a "Hilfsvokal" before the fricative sequence */hw/- (he writes /χw/). In making this identification he brings this type of prothesis into line with the other type mentioned in 1.0 and exemplified by Grk. ἰχθύς = Arm. ǰukn, and hence requires but one type of prothesis. Although assuming prothesis before */hw/- < */sw/- does not require inventing new entities, it is excluded by the facts of Grk. phonology, for */sw/- quite clearly develops to /h/- in ἀνδάνω 'please', ἡδύς 'sweet' < *swād- and ἥν 'her' < *swēn. And if a vowel were to have developed before */hw/- < */sw/-, one imagines that it would further have developed to V̄, as in the case of νᾱός 'temple' < *naswos and εὕαδε (= ἥαδε) < *eswade.

Nikitina (1962:83-85) also allows a connection of prothesis with */s/-, but before all sonants, and in so doing connects ἀείρω with German schwer 'heavy' from IE *swer-, and ὀλισθάνω 'slip, slide', with OE slidan. But there is this difference between Nikitina's position and Crossland's: Nikitina (1962:85-86) assumes an alternation in these roots between laryngeal and */s/-,

---

[7] Beekes (1969:18-98) has provided the fullest recent discussion of laryngeal origin of prothesis. He not only discusses all earlier views — more thoroughly than I have — but has also carefully sifted alleged cases of initial laryngeal in Grk. words which later appear with prothetic vowel. His work is therefore highly useful, but in the end, since he follows Austin (1941) and Cowgill (1965) in the main, contributes nothing of theoretical importance.

thus writing for the roots just mentioned *swer- ≈ *Hwer- and *slei- ≈ *Hlei-, and implying that Grk. prothesis results from the vocalized laryngeal, while cognate forms like schwer and slidan continue the form with */s/-. This solution lacks the neatness and simplicity of Crossland's, even though it does get around the */sw/- > */hw/- > /h/- objection. It is, though, subject to all the objections raised above to other laryngeal explanations.[8] It seems that prothesis cannot result from a vowel developing either before /h/-, whether from IE */s/- or from an IE laryngeal, or from the laryngeal /h/- itself.

One scholar held that prothesis, though a development of an IE phenomenon, does not involve laryngeals. A. Cuny (1943: 57-111, discussed by Lejeune 1943:137-149) held that "nostratic," the language ancestral to both IE and Hamito-Semitic, possessed two series of resonant consonants, the emphatic (*R L M N W Y), and the unemphatic (*r l m n w y). Prothesis in Grk. developed before the emphatic consonants and only there, while the unemphatic consonants were everywhere continued by the simple resonants. Thus ἐλεύθερος 'free' < *Leudh-, while λευκός 'light, bright, clear' < *leuk-. This theory, refuted in detail by Lejeune, starts off with two drawbacks: its support comes from but one IE language, and its theoretical necessity has to do with a non-IE language. That is, it came into being because of Cuny's belief that IE and Hamito-Semitic are related, and derives its evidential support only from Grk. within the IE family. These facts, added to the theory's inability to account for cases like ἀλείφω : λίπος, make it as untenable as theories operating with

---

[8] It also encounters difficulties with IE root theory, as indeed do many instances of laryngeal explanations. Most laryngealists feel, following Benveniste (1935:146-173), that the IE root contained a maximum of five morphophonemes, CeCeC, which could appear in one of two forms, either as stage I CeCC-, or as stage II CCeC-. Clearly *Hleidh-, *Hmelg- and *Hmeig- (Chantraine 1968:74) have too many consonants, since morphophonemically they are all CeCeCeC. And, as Lejeune (1943:133) points out, laryngeal in *wel- 'wish' is excluded because stage II *wlep-, seen in Lat. lepos 'charm' beside stage I *welp- in Grk. ἔλπω, proves that the root can have been nothing other than *wel-.

laryngeals. Nonetheless, as we shall see below (6.0), phonetically Cuny came very close to being right.

I know of no one who feels that prothesis originated in a generalization of sentence phonetics within IE, though such could be imagined without much difficulty. All the consonants involved appear in IE languages in two forms, as (e.g.) [m] and as [m̥], which in Grk. itself develop to /m/ and /am/ respectively (and to /n r l w/ and /an ar al uw/ respectively). It is clear enough that [m] occurs between vowels and after a single consonant, and that [m̥] occurs between consonants and between consonant and pause. But it might well be that [m̥] would occur (in the form [m̥m] > /am/) also before a vowel if preceded by two consonants (Edgerton 1943). Thus -/nt m/- might be realized phonetically as [ntm̥m] > Grk. [ntam]. And this particular sandhi variant might have been generalized. An explanation of this sort would clearly have the advantage of being able to explain doublets (like ἀλείφω : λίπος; μαλακός : ἀμαλός), but it has the disadvantage of being unable to explain the color of the prothetic vowel before /w/- and the apparently universal occurrence of prothesis before /r/-. Furthermore it is obviously an ad hoc explanation which by explaining too much explains too little.

If one were to seek a morphological explanation for Grk. prothesis in terms of inherited IE words, one would do so by appealing to one of the numerous prefixes */a/- < *[n̥]. But here of course the difficulty arises that cognates in other languages should also appear with the same prefix in order to posit an IE origin, and if they do not, one should rather assume that the compounds were formed in Grk. times. We shall accordingly mention most of these possibilities in connection with explanations based on Grk. material. But one or two attempts at IE morphological explanation might be mentioned here. Winter (1950) explains prothesis as resulting from doubly dissimilated reduplications in a number of cases, and in ἀγείρω 'bring together' and ἀκαρός· σημαίνει τὸν ἐγκέφαλον ἢ τὴν κεφαλήν (EM) at least as continuing an IE prefix *n̥ 'together with' (Winter 1952: 186-191). But none of the cases he discusses involve resonants, and his explanations are therefore not of interest to us here:

before resonants he allows laryngeal origin, at least in some forms (Winter 1965a:202-203). Seiler (1957), though, does explain "prothesis" before a resonant (in ἀλέγω 'have a care', ἀλίγκιος 'resembling, like', ἄμοτον 'insatiably') as the continuation of an earlier prefix $*\overset{n}{\underset{o}{}}$, this $*\overset{n}{\underset{o}{}}$ being the reduced grade of the preposition $*en$ 'in'. He is reluctant to attribute this form of the preposition to IE because there are no cognates of it elsewhere (Seiler 1957:22-23), but he does assign it at least to proto-Greek. The assumption of such a prefix is not impossible, but unfortunately it does not account for the most striking cases of prothesis, and in fact accounts only for words which have in the past been explained without the assumption of prothesis.

1.1.2 Turning now to prothesis as a Grk. innovation, we find in general the same possibilities, though here the phonotactic seems a good deal less likely (cf. Lejeune 1955:129, 273; Schwyzer 1939:412-413). Though admitting a number of different possibilities for an explanation of prothesis, Lejeune (1955:181) seems to hold that prothesis is a Grk. development only, or if not that, a development restricted to Grk. and Arm. and Alb., and at that a peculiarly phonetic development (1955:181; examples of prothesis: 127-129, 148). He feels that general phonetics can explain prothesis and that it need not be an inherited phenomenon. Schwyzer (1939:412) mentions two views of the origin of prothesis. The usual view, he says, is that prothesis originated through early onset of voice at the beginning of a sentence: "verfrühtes Einsetzen des Stimmtons im Satzanlaut oder ähnlich." He himself favors epenthesis of a vowel after a consonant as in the German dialect of Wallis where *das ist recht* is phonetically *dašt^a recht* (in his notation). But neither of these explanations is plausible because neither explains why prothesis was generalized in those words in which it occurs and not in others with the same initial consonant. That an epenthetic vowel might develop under such conditions is possible — though consonantal assimilation seems in fact to have been the normal Grk. rule (Lejeune 1955:281-285) — but that it should be generalized from this one special environment to all environments is on the whole most unlikely. And this is in general the difficulty with all phonetic explanations: to the assumption that a prothetic vowel develops regularly before a consonant by purely phonetic pressures it must be objected that the precise phonetic conditions under which it arises have not been isolated. Hence the feeling that prothesis arose in Grk. by phonetic means is, as formulated, not sufficiently explicit to command attention. We shall see below, however, that, given the proper limitations, it is in fact correct.

A morphological explanation of prothesis in Grk. would hold that all cases of so-called prothesis are in fact compounds of either of the prefixes ἀ- (negative prefix in ἀληθής 'true'; copulative in ἄλοχος 'wife'), ἐ- (the prefix in ἐθέλω beside θέλω 'be willing', ἐκεῖνος beside κεῖνος 'that one'; the augment in ἔλιπον beside λείπω 'leave'), or ὀ- (copulative in ὄπατρος 'having the same father'; local in the meaning 'nearly' in ὀκέλλω 'run aground' beside κέλλω 'drive on'). And indeed such prefixes do occur with considerable frequency in Grk. and one has always to allow for them, but they cannot explain the vast majority of cases of vowel prothesis. And in order for any one of them to be assumed, there should be semantic evidence that the prefix is present, i.e., the meaning of the word should support the assumption of prefixation. These prefixes serve, therefore, to provide a limit on the numbers of cases of prothesis, but do not provide an explanation for prothesis in general.

1.1.3 It is now time to present my own explanation for prothesis, an explanation which falls squarely into the second category: I feel that the prothetic vowel developed in Grk. alone as a result of purely Grk. phonological rules and tendencies. For the present I would formulate my rule as a regularity only, and hold that: a (prothetic) vowel of undetermined timbre (we may assume [ə]) arises only (but not always) before /l m n w/ when /l m n w/ are followed by a short vowel in a syllable closed either by a resonant or semivowel plus consonant, or by a consonant plus resonant or semivowel. We may symbolize this rule provisionally as follows:

$$\text{RVRC-} \rightarrow \text{əRVRC-}$$
$$\text{RVCR-} \rightarrow \text{əRVCR-}$$

Modifications and further specifications will be provided for this regularity later on. Since it would be relatively easy to provide ample support for this regularity if I were to choose only my own positive examples, I shall in the next chapter utilize only those examples which have been most commonly accepted and which are listed by Lejeune (1955:127-129, 148) and Schwyzer (1939: 411-412). I shall signify which of them favors which examples by means of the abbreviations L. and S. Other possible positive instances will be reserved for the third chapter.

WIDELY ACCEPTED CASES OF PROTHESIS

2. Widely accepted cases of prothesis include:

2.1.1. (L.S.) ἀλείτης (*Il.* 3.28) 'sinner', fem. ἀλεῖτις (Hdn. *Gr.* 2.67) and with the o-grade ἀλοίτης (Emp. 10) 'avenger' Ἀλοῖτις (Lyc. 936), an epithet of Athena, ἀλοιτός = ἀλείτης (Lyc. 136), fem. ἀλοιταί· κοιναί ἁμαρτωλαί, ποιναί (Hsch.).[9] Beside these nominal forms there also exists the large family of verbal forms and derivatives in ἀλιτ- which includes ἀλιταίνω, ἤλιτον (epic) 'sin against', ἀλιτρός 'sinful' (*Il.* 8.361 — for ἀλειτρός? cf. νηλειτίδες, v.l. νηλιτίδες), ἀλιτήριος 'sinning against' (Ar. *Eq.* 445). There are no forms of this root in Grk. without prothesis, though from the distribution supposed in 1.1.3 above we should expect prothesis only before heavy syllables, and hence *λιταίνω λιτεῖν. The simplest way to account for this discrepancy between expectation and occurrence is to assume that prothesis arose first in the noun ἀλείτης and spread thence to the verb *λιτεῖν : ἀλείτης → ἀλιτεῖν : ἀλείτης. Etymologically, this group of words is ordinarily

---

[9] The punctuation in the text is that of K. Latte (*Hesychii Alexandrini Lexicon* I.113 [Copenhagen, 1953]), but LSJ put a comma between the first two words of the gloss, and this is more likely to be correct. Then, if we take ἁμαρτωλαί to be the feminine of ἁμαρτωλός, we can translate the first two words: 'prostitutes' (LSJ IV 3c), 'sinners'. The third gloss then presents difficulties as it stands, but the emendation to πόρναι lies ready to hand and is palaeographically easy (H. C. Youtie, *The Textual Criticism of Documentary Papyri: Prolegomena,* Bulletin of the Institute of Classical Studies of the University of London, Suppl. 6 p. 69 [London, 1958]; cf. also C. H. Roberts, *Greek Literary Hands* 21a [Oxford, 1956]). The whole notion of ἀλοιταί as πόρναι may well go back to Odysseus' maids who slept with the suitors (*Od.* 22.417ff.)

connected with OHG *leid,* ON *leiðr* 'unangenehm, verhasst' (Frisk 1.67, Chantraine 1968:56-57).[10]

2.1.2 (L.S.) ἀλείφω 'anoint with oil' (Frisk 1.67-68, Chantraine 1968:57) is, despite Beekes' objections (1969:40) connected with λίπος 'animal fat', and both in turn are cognate with Skt. *limpati* 'smear' (Frisk 2.126-127). Other forms of this same root to occur in early times are ἄλειφαρ (*Il.* 18.351), ἄλειφα (Hes. *Th.* 553) 'unguent', Mycenaean *a-re-pa-te* (PY Un 267) 'unguent', *a-re-pa-zo-o* (PY Un 267) *a-re-po-zo-o* (Ea 812) 'unguent-boiler' (Chadwick 1963:169-170), ἀλοιφή (*Il.* 9.208) 'grease'. Later there occur ἄλειψις (Hdt. 3.22) 'an anointing' and ἄλειμμα (Plat. *Ti.* 50e) 'fat'. The verb itself has the principle parts ἀλείψω (E. *IA* 1486), ἤλειφα (*Il.* 18.350) ἀλήλιφα (D. 52.29), ἀλήλιμμαι (Th. 4.68). Thus all early forms of this word (save λίπος) have a syllable closed by /i/ following the /l/, thus conforming to the rule. And λίπος also conforms to the rule because prothesis is not to be expected before an open syllable /li/-.

2.1.3 (L.S.) Certainly connected with the preceding word, and possibly influenced by it, is ἀλίνειν· ἀλείφειν, ἀλῖναι· ἐπαλεῖψαι (Hsch.), ἰναλαλισμένα 'engraved, inscribed' (Cyprus: Schwyzer 1923:679.26), ἄλινσις = ἄλειψις (*IG* 4.1484.39 — Epidaurus). Extra-Greek cognates include Lat. *lino* 'besmear' and Skt. (gramm.) *lināti* 'sich anschmiegen'. All of these forms indicate that the earliest reconstructible form of the Grk. word, if indeed it dates from proto-Greek times, is *linyō (or *leinyō). But it is not as yet possible to state at what phonological stage in the history of the Greek language prothesis developed, so that it could have originated before *linyō, *lihnō (cf. Kiparsky 1968), *linnō or *līnō (= /liyno/?). Or it could simply have been

---

[10] There seems to be no prothesis-less form of ἀλιτεῖν. But it might well be that λιτή 'prayer', λιτέσθαι 'pray' is such a form and that the two words diverged later on. If so, λιτή must have meant 'offense' originally, and λιτεῖν 'commit an offense', λιτέσθαι 'admit an offense' or some such. For a similar semantic relation one thinks of ἀρά which means both 'prayer' and 'curse'. And the double function of the Λιταί in *Il.* 9.502-512 — both curers and summoners of ἄτη — becomes easier to understand.

extended by analogy from ἀλείφω, a possibility so distinct that ἀλίνω cannot be considered secure independent evidence for relevant environments for the development of prothesis.

2.1.4 (L.S.) ἐλαφρός (*Il.* 12.450) 'light in weight'. Though there are numerous derivatives of this word, all show the same stem form ἐλαφρ-, and there is therefore no need or point to listing them here. Frisk (1.484) connects this word with OHG *lungar*, OS *lungor* 'schnell', OE *lungre* 'schnell, bald' and derives all from an IE *l̥ŋgᵂhros. Schwyzer's suggestion (1939:302) that ἐλαφρός derives from a contamination of *ἐλαχρός (< *l̥ŋgᵂhros = OHG *lungar*) and *ἐλαφός (< *ἐλαχϝός = Lith. *lengvas* 'leicht') is unnecessary, since *-ghwr- merged with -gᵂhr- and hence developed along with it to -pʰr-. But whatever the word's precise history, the /l/ is always followed by a vowel in a closed syllable, and no forms without prothesis occur. It is most likely that this word was the original positive to the comparative of the following example.[11]

2.1.5 (L.) ἐλαχύς (Nic. *Th.* 324), fem. ἐλάχεια (v.l. to λάχεια *Od.* 9.116, 10.509, *h.Ap.* 197), ntr. ἐλαχύ (*AP* 7.498), ἔλαχος = ἐλαχύς (Call. *Fr.* 349) 'small, short', comp. ἐλάσσων (*Il.* 10.357) 'smaller, less', the semantic comparative, not to ἐλαχύς, but to μικρός; superlative ἐλάχιστος (*h.Merc.* 573) 'smallest, least'. Again there are numerous derivatives, some early, but again, too, the root form is constant throughout. But there is some difficulty with the form ἐλαχύς itself which may well be a late back-formation from ἐλάσσων since the masc. and ntr. forms are attested at the earliest in Alexandrian times. The feminine form, though, occurs early and merits a somewhat longer discussion.

The relevant passages are:

Od. 9.116-117:   Νῆσος ἔπειτα λάχεια παρὲκ λιμένος τετάνυσται
                   γαίης Κυκλώπων οὔτε σχέδον οὔτ' ἀποτηλοῦ

Od. 10.508-509: ἀλλ' ὁπότ' ἂν δὴ νηὶ δι' Ὠκεάνοιο περήσῃς
                   ἔνθ' ἀκτή τε λάχεια καὶ ἄλσεα Περσεφονείης

---

[11] For the possibility of a relation of this sort (-ρος, -ίων, -ιστος) cf. Seiler 1950:74-79, Kühner-Blass 1890:556, Schwyzer 1939:536-539.

h.Ap. 197-199:   τῆσι μὲν οὔτ' αἰσχρὴ μεταμέλπεται οὔτε λάχεια,

ἀλλὰ μάλα μεγάλη τε ἰδεῖν καὶ εἶδος ἀγητή,

Ἄρτεμις ἰοχέαιρα ὁμότροφος Ἀπόλλωνι

In all these passages λάχεια is the best attested reading, but also in all these passages, ἐλάχεια can be read. And indeed Leumann (1950:54) has assumed that ἐλάχεια is the correct reading. But his argument is not convincing, based as it is on the a priori expectation that the positive to a comparative ἐλάσσων should be ἐλαχύς ἐλάχεια, as indeed it should be if the comparative was formed to the positive. But since ἐλάσσων is the comparative to μικρός and had become separated from (ἐ)λαχύς, it is just as likely that ἐλαχύς ἐλάχεια replace an earlier *λαχύς *λάχεια under the influence of ἐλάσσων ἐλάχιστος. Thus, though the meaning of λάχεια in the *Odyssey* passages is not altogether clear,[12] we are probably justified in accepting the better-attested variant, and assuming an original comparative scheme: *laghus* (< *l̥nghus*) *laghyōn* *laghistos* which became in Grk. *λαχύς *ἐλάχγων λάχιστος → λαχύς ἐλάσσων ἐλάχιστος, this last with the ἐ- analogically brought over from ἐλάσσων.[13] Because λαχύς (if the

---

[12] LSJ glosses the word as 'small, short, mean, little', a meaning that does not well suit either of the *Odyssey* passages. But if we remember that in both cases the land is approached from the sea, it may be that the word means 'short' in the sense that there is little distance between the water-line and the end of the beach. In *Od.* 9.116-117 the island may have been low-lying, and indeed may have been in the nature of a sand-bar and not a real island at all. To be sure the passage indicates otherwise, but the details of the island may be a later addition to the passage, an addition prompted by mariners' reports and geographical speculation (cf. Carpenter 1946:103-105). On this assumption at an earlier stage lines 116-117 might have been followed by lines 140ff. Support for this interpretation can be gleaned from the Heraclean tables (Schwyzer 1923:19-28) where we read in 1.38: τὰν δὲ νᾶσον τὰν ποτιγεγενημέναν ἐς τὰν ἄρρηκτον γᾶν συνεμετρήσαμες where νᾶσον is clearly an alluvial deposit of obviously no great height or extent. If we take νῆσος in *Od.* 9.116 to have meant originally 'sand-bar', we both provide a semantic link between the two *Odyssey* passages, and also gain an idea of the original meaning of λάχεια. It meant 'small' (when seen from the open sea).

[13] Further support for the assumption that the comparative is the more original form of this word in Grk. can be derived from the large number of

positive was not in fact ἐλαφρός) fell out of use early on it did not receive the prothetic ἐ- until Callimachus created ἐλαχύς (and ἔλαχος!) on the basis of ἐλάσσων ἐλάχιστος and the assumption that he was by so doing recovering an ancient form. If the above reasoning is correct, then we find the regularity given above once again supported: prothesis develops only before a closed syllable (*lakhy-) beginning with a resonant.

2.1.6 (L.) ἐλεύθερος (Il. 6.455) 'free', Mycenaean e-re-u-te-ro (PY Na 248), e-re-u-te-ra (PY Na 106) 'free', e-re-u-te-ro-se (PY Na 395) = ἐλευθέρωσε, 'made free' (Chadwick 1963:190). This word is clearly related to Lat. liber 'free' and OHG liut 'people', as well as to numerous other IE words meaning 'people, folk' (Frisk 1.490-491).

2.1.7 (S.) ὀλίγος (Il. +) 'little, few, small' clearly constitutes an exception to my rule, as do all the numerous derivatives of this word, as well as the superlative ὀλίγιστος (Il. 19.223), for which to be sure, we could read: ἄμητος δὲ λίγιστος. But again the comparative comes through with a closed syllable: though the comparative of ὀλίγος is ordinarily supplied by μείων, ἥσσων or ἐλάσσων, the form ὀλίζων occurs in Alexandrian poets and already in Il. 18.519 in the phrase: λαοὶ δ᾽ ὑπ᾽ ὀλίζονες (or ὀλείζονες: LSJ) ἦσαν; and the Attic form ὀλείζων occurs in IG 1².76.8 (ὀλεῖζον ibid. 63.17 and elsewhere), ὀλείζοσι (ibid. 6.76), and ὀλείζους is probable in Xen. Ath. 2.1 for the μείζους of the manuscripts (so Bowersock HSCP 71[1967]50 following Wilamowitz). The relation between these forms is not absolutely clear, but Seiler (1950:101-102) has supposed that these forms stand to each other as does Ionic μέζων to Attic μείζων, that is, that ὀλίζων > ὀλέζων after its antonym μείζων (=[me:dzɔ:n]). He may of course be right, but from my point of view and for my argument it would be best to assume *leigyōn > *oleigyōn, for then the syllable would be closed by a semivowel as it has been generally

---

derivatives formed from it and the absence of derivatives of Grk. ἐλαχύς. There is also the more general consideration that there are more comparatives in -(ι)ων than positives to match them. Cf. the table in Seiler 1950:34.

in the cases thus far discussed.[14] But *ligyōn would not be impossible in terms of the hypothesis framed in 1.1.3 above (cf. *lakhyōn > ἐλάσσων), for the syllable is still closed, this time by some sort of affricate. But if we adopt *leigyōn (or even *ligyōn), we then are forced to assume, if we wish to preserve our hypothesis, that at one time *oleigyōn was far more common than it was in classical times, and that both the positive and the superlative received the prothetic vowel from this *oleigyōn. I am willing to make that assumption.[15]

[14] Supporting the notion that ὀλείζων is correct and ὀλίζων formed after ὀλίγος are two considerations, neither one unconditionally convincing. 1) It is difficult to see how ὀλίζων → ὀλέζων etc. after μέγας : μείζων (=[me:dzɔ:n], for the parallelism is not there: rather we should expect ὀλίζων on the assumption of a rule: in comparatives in -ων lengthen the vowel in the syllable immediately preceding -ων. 2) In PIE, whatever the ablaut grade of the positive, the comparative degree always contained the strong grade (Seiler 1950:22): hence from the point of view of PIE we should expect ὀλείζων. I shall continue to assume that *leigyōn was the proto-Grk. form before which prothesis developed. Another factor in favor of assuming *leig- rather than *lig- has to do with the very phenomenon of prothesis itself. The vowel quality of the prothetic vowel is /o/- in this group of words, and as we shall see, /o/- seems the quality favored before /ei/ (cf. ὀμείχω — 2.2.3, ὄνειδος — 2.3.1, οἴγνυμι — 2.4.13), though not before /i/.

[15] Frisk (2.376 and particularly 2.134) connects ὀλίγος with λοιγός 'ruin, destruction' and thus further with Lith. líegti 'schwer krank sein, siechen', Alb. lig 'böse, mager' and Arm. aǐkʻ-at 'arm, dürftig', none of which is really very likely or plausible. Another possibility for an etymological identification might be mentioned, though I fear that it is no more likely than Frisk's explanation, and will not succeed in finding any IE cognates for ὀλίγος. Comparatives in -ων have as their positive a wide variety of stem types (Kühner-Blass 1890:554-557), but one of the most frequent is u-stem adjectives such as ἡδύς ἡδίων 'sweet', βραχύς βράσσων 'short' (Seiler 1950:35-62). If we take our cue from this type of relation, we would be moved to posit λιγύς (or de rigueur *λιδύς) as the original positive of ὀλ(ε)ίζων, and would then assume that ὀλίγος was abstracted from ὀλ(ε)ίζων at a later date (cf. Callimachus' ἐλαχύς and ἔλαχος, both abstracted from ἐλάσσων ἐλάχιστος — 2.1.5 above). And of course there is a Grk. word λιγύς 'shrill, sharp' which could have been the original positive. Clearly the semantic link is weak in such a connection, but it may not be insurmountable if we recall that a low note was by the Greeks

2.1.8 Schwyzer, but not Lejeune, includes ὀλόπτω 'pluck out, tear out' which occurs in the phrases [χαίτην] ὤλοψας βίηφι (Call. *Dian.* 77) and ἐὰν ὠλόψατο χαίτην (*AP* 7.241), and in the Hesychian gloss ὀλόπτειν· λεπίζειν, τίλλειν, κολάπτειν. The second two of these glosses suit well the Callimachus and *AP* passages, while the first, λεπίζειν, works well for the meaning 'strip off' (Nic. *Th.* 595). Schwyzer's assumption (1939:411), and Frisk's (2.381), too, is that this word is connected in some way with λέπω 'peel, strip', λοπός 'peel', and Frisk, indeed, regards ὀλόπτω as the causative to λέπω, a rather strange supposition, for to a λέπω λοπός, if a causative should be required, we would expect *λοπέω, or the actually occuring λεπίζω and λωπίζω. There seems no place for a causative *λόπτω, and what is more, this derivation leaves out of account the glosses of Hesychius: ὀλούφειν (ms. ὀλουφεῖν)· τίλλειν and διολουφεῖν· διατίλλειν ἢ διασιλλαίνειν. Detracting further from the weight to be attributed to these forms is the fact that they are attested only in the Alexandrian period at the earliest, a period in which verbs in -πτω were experiencing a great vogue (Debrunner 1907:207-214, Schwyzer 1939:704-705). Hence ὀλόπτω runs the risk of being a late form created by poets on λέπω (or λοπός, or even λόφος 'crest') and therefore not a true case of prothesis.[16]

---

considered to be heavy, βαρύς, to which they opposed the high tone 'sharp', ὀξύς. Possibly they at one time opposed 'heavy' to 'small, light' = 'high, shrill', λιγύς. Subsequently, on this assumption, λιγύς 'small, high, shrill' became specialized in the sense of 'shrill', while its comparative ὀλείζων went the other way, becoming specialized in the meaning 'smaller'. To this comparative in this meaning was then formed the new positive ὀλίγος. Hesychius' glosses: λίζον· ἔλαττον, λίζονες· ἐλάττονες show the regular development of *λιγ-: prothesis develops before /i/+consonant only when that consonant is aspirated. More on this in 5.9.1 below.

[16] A further objection to the inclusion of these words here, and indeed the only important objection from my point of view, is that both are unusual in containing an /o/ in the root syllable. In all previous instances we have found that the /o/ vowel occurred only in derivatives showing e ∽ o ablaut, and will see later that /o/ nowhere allows prothesis. We might expect a similar relation here. And Frisk (2.382) records a suggestion of Grošelj that ὀλούφειν is

2.1.9 On the basis of the examples of prothesis accepted by Schwyzer and Lejeune and of the discussions above we can make the following general statements in rule form expressed in terms of the following vowel (ə represents the developing prothesis):

i) $*le\begin{bmatrix}i\\u\end{bmatrix}C$-   → $*əle\begin{bmatrix}i\\u\end{bmatrix}C$-

ἀλείτης ἀλείφω ἐλεύθερος [ὀλείζων]

ii) $*la\begin{bmatrix}p^h\\k^h\end{bmatrix}\begin{bmatrix}r\\y\end{bmatrix}$-   → $*əla\begin{bmatrix}p^h\\k^h\end{bmatrix}\begin{bmatrix}r\\y\end{bmatrix}$-

ἐλαφρός ἐλάσσων

iii) $*liCy$-   → $*əliCy$-

ἀλίνω [ὀλίζων]

Prothesis does not occur before /o/ in the root syllable (unless we include ὀλόπτειν ὀλούφειν) save in roots in which it had developed already before /e/: ἀλοίτης ἀλοιφή; nor does it occur before /u/. And a more general formulation governing prothesis before /l/ would be: initial */l/ followed by a non-rounded vowel in a syllable closed either by a semivowel or resonant followed by a consonant, or a consonant followed by a semivowel or resonant, develops a vocalic onset of uncertain color (prothetic vowel). And then schematically (R = resonant, C = any consonant):

$$*l\begin{bmatrix}e\\a\\i\end{bmatrix}\begin{bmatrix}RC\\CR\end{bmatrix}\text{-} \quad \rightarrow \quad *əl\begin{bmatrix}e\\a\\i\end{bmatrix}\begin{bmatrix}RC\\CR\end{bmatrix}\text{-}$$

2.2.0 The rule just given works for */l/, but there is no very good reason to suppose that it will work also for */m/, for it is quite clear that */r/ and */y/ at least behave differently: perhaps */m/, and nasals generally, do not behave in the same way as the lateral /l/, even though both are also members of R(esonant).

---

connected with Lat. *liber* 'book', Russ. *lub* 'bast', and that all derive from an IE *l(e)ubh-. If this attractive suggestion is adopted, then we can imagine the development: *leubho > *əleubho > *ἐλεύφω → *ὀλουφός → ὀλουφεῖν. This word influenced λέπτω to develop a by-form ὀλόπτω.

Again I shall discuss only those instances of prothesis that are accepted by Schwyzer and Lejeune. I will start with those which do conform to the regularity given in 1.1.3, and will then pass to cases which are more problematic from my point of view.

2.2.1 (S.) ἀμείβω 'change' ἀμοιβή 'exchange'. Schwyzer connects this root with Lat. *migrare* 'wander', and though Frisk (1.90) feels that this is not a certain connection, it is the only one suggested that has any plausibility. Chantraine (1968:73-74) adds only Skt. *ni-máyate* 'exchange' and Lat. *munus* 'gift'. The word conforms completely to the formula: ReRC- > əReRc- given for */l/ above.

2.2.2 (S.L.) ἀμέλγω 'milk' ἀμολγός '?' (Frisk 1.94) ἀμολγή 'a milking'. The o-grade derivatives of this root are rare and in part uncertain, but extra-Greek cognates are both many and certain for the e-grade (Frisk 1.91), among them Eng. *milk*, and all point to an IE root *melg- which developed to *əmelg- in proto-Greek.

2.2.3 (S.L.) ὀμείχω (Hes. *E*. 727: codd. ὀμιχεῖν), ὀμεῖξαι (Hippon. 55A: codd. -ι- or -η-), ἀμῖξαι· οὐρῆσαι (Hsch.) 'make water'. This obviously IE word has numerous cognates in other languages, all pointing to a root *meigh-: Skt. *mehati*, Ave. *maēzaiti*, Lat. *meio, mingo*, all meaning 'make water' (Frisk 2.385). Clearly this word conforms to the rule I have established, and for the first time we find other than statistical support for excluding /o/ in the root syllable as one of the vowels allowing prothesis to develop. For, though etymological connection cannot be considered certain, it does appear most likely that Frisk (2.249-250) is correct in assuming that μοιχός 'adulterer' is related to ὀμείχω. The reason for the different treatment of the initial, unknown to Frisk, is that prothesis does not develop before resonant followed by /o/.

2.2.4 (L.S.) ὀμίχλη (*Il*. 1.359) 'mist, fog', and possibly ἀμιχ-θαλόεσσαν (*Il*. 24.753), meaning unknown, is clearly related to a number of IE words meaning 'fog' (Frisk 2.387): Lith. *miglà*, OCS *migla*, Skt. *mih-* 'fog, haze', *meghá-* 'cloud'. But in spite of a seeming semantic similarity, it does not appear that ὀμείχω is to be connected with this word (the velars differ), though I should not want to exclude connection completely, even if only on the level of folk etymology.

2.2.5 ἀμαλός (*Il.* 22.310) 'soft, weak' has been connected by Lejeune with ἀμαλδύνω (*Il.* 7.463) 'destroy' and μαλακός (*Il.* 1.582) 'soft' beside μέλδομαι (21.363) 'make liquid'; he further adduces as extra-Greek cognates: Skt. *mṛduḥ* 'soft, tender', Lat. *mollis* 'soft', Arm. *mełk* 'schlaff'. Though ἀμαλδύνω fits easily into the category of prothetic forms, clearly ἀμαλός does not, for prothesis should occur only in closed syllables, and ἀμαλός therefore (from my point of view) requires a different explanation. Beekes (1969:44), indeed, feels that "there is insufficient reason to speak of a prothetic vowel." Lejeune's list of cognates must be extended before we can approach an explanation. Including those words mentioned by Lejeune, the following are usually considered in connection with ἀμαλός.

a) Words with initial ἀ-:

1)	ἀμαλός	'soft, weak'
2)	ἀμαλδύνω	'soften' (QS 1.73), 'crush, destroy' (*Il.* 12.18)
3)	ἀμβλύς	'blunt, dulled' (A. *Eu.* 238)

b) Words with initial β- (1-4 from Hsch.):

1)	βλαδαρόν· ἐκλελυμένον χαῦνον	
2)	βλαδεῖς· ἀδύνατοι, ἐξ ἀδυνάτων	
3)	βλάδαν· νωθρῶς	
4)	βλαδόν· ἀδύνατον	
5)	βλάξ	'stolid, stupid' (Pl. *Grg.* 488a)
6)	βληχρός	'faint, gentle' (Alc. 16)
7)	ἀβληχρός	'weak, feeble' (*Il.* 5.337)

c) Words with initial μ-:

1)	μαλακός	'soft, cowardly, gentle' (*Il.* 1.582)
2)	μαλθακός	'soft, gentle' (*Il.* 17.588)
3)	μέλδομαι	'soften by boiling' (*Il.* 21.363)
4)	μύλη	'mill' (*Od.* 7.104)
5)	μῶλυς	'soft, weak' (S. *Fr.* 693)

All these words (save ἀμαλδύνω and μύλη) share a meaning 'soft, dull, weak', i.e., 'not up to standard', and, since all the words in b) are to be treated as having derived from *ml-, phonologically the consonants /m/ and /l/, and a vowel, long or short, before or after the /l/. For the rest, things are unclear, though it seems that at least two, and probably more likely three, base forms are required.

1) *mldu-, connected with Lat. mollis and Skt. mṛdú-, lies behind ἀμαλδύνω (< *mldu- > *maldu- > *amaldu-) and the first four words in b);

2) *mlā-, connected with Skt. mlātá- 'soft' and OIr mláith 'gentle, soft' (< *mlā-ti-) is the original form of βλάξ βληχρός ἀβληχρός (for *ἀμβληχρος in b); as well as for μαλακός μαλθακός in c) if one is willing to accept here an alternation -lā- ∼ -ala-.

3)*mlu, probably a by-form of *mlā-, provides the root for ἀμβλύς and μῶλυς. We are then left with μέλδομαι, which as we shall see later derives from *smeld-; and μύλη, which is probably not connected with any of the above, but rather with Lat. molō 'grind'; and ἀμαλός. There are any number of possibilities for this word, prothesis of course among them, and they include analogy with ἀμβλύς or ἀμαλδύνω, as well as the zero grade of a long vocalic root: "deutlich hängt der Vokal von ἀμβλύς gegenüber μῶλυς mit dem Anlaut von ἀμαλός zusammen" (Schwyzer 1939: 363). But perhaps the strongest possibility of all, since ἀμαλός fits neither with my rule nor (comfortably) with any of the root forms listed above, is that ἀμαλός is a vox nihili, a form created by the poets as a result of a syntactic error. The word occurs only twice in Homer:

Il. 22.309: ὅς τ᾽ εἶσιν πεδίονδε διὰ νεφέων ἐρεβεννῶν
ἁρπάξων ἢ ἄρν᾽ ἀμαλὴν ἢ πτῶκα λαγωόν

Od. 20.14: ὡς δὲ κύων ἀμαλῇσι περὶ σκυλάκεσσι βεβῶσα
ἄνδρ᾽ ἀγνοιήσασ᾽ ὑλάει μέμονέν τε μάχεσθαι

in the second passage at least clearly referring to young animals (v.l. ἀπαλῇσι). In the first passage 'young, small' vel sim. would do, but is not required (v.1. ἄρνα μάλην = 'white lamb' or 'tender lamb'). If we were to adopt the variant readings, we could destroy the Homeric attestation of this word, but we are prevented from so doing by Euripides' use of the word (*Heracl.* 75):

ἴδετε τὸν γέροντ᾽ ἀμαλὸν ἐπὶ πέδῳ

χύμενον· ὦ τάλας

a reading vouched for by Hesychius' ἀμαλόν· ἀπαλόν, ἀσθενῆ. Εὐριπίδης Ἡρακλείδαις δηλοῖ. And Callimachus (*Fr.* 502P) seems to use the word in this sense: ἦν μο(ύ)νη ῥύετο παῖς ἀμαλή. But the variant readings and the uncertainty of the word's meaning reflected by the ancient scholia do indicate that the ancients themselves were really at a loss to explain the word, thus indicating the possibility at least that connection with μαλακός was born of desperation, and that the word is to be explained in some other way.

There is another word in Grk. of similar shape which also refers to the young of animals, though it is restricted generally to young cows. I refer to δάμαλις (A. *Supp.* 351) 'heifer' beside δαμάλη (E. *Ba.* 739, Theoc. 4.12, *POxy.* 1734.2), and the masculine forms δαμάλης (Arist. *HA* 632ª15) and δάμαλος (Hdn. *Gr.* 1.159). But the most important attestation for our purposes is the phrase δάμαλις σῦς (*IG* 5(1).1390.34, 69 — Andania) dating from the first century B.C., a phrase which proves that δάμαλις (to δαμάζω — Frisk 1.345) originally could refer to the young of any (domestic) animal. And δάμαλις must be the particularizing feminine to an adjective δάμαλος δαμαλη (accent uncertain) or δαμάλης (Chantraine 1933:237-238) just as ἡμερίς 'the cultivated one', hence 'the vine', is the feminine of ἥμερος 'cultivated, tame'. Not only do these words share similarities in word formation, they are similar semantically as well: δαμαλος meant 'the (to be) tamed', and to it was a formed a particularizing feminine δάμαλις 'the one (to be) tamed'. The Homeric ἀμαλός can then be simply a truncated form of δαμαλος interpreted semantically in terms of the supposed synonym ἀπαλός (from which it may have derived its accent) and formally in terms of its near homonym μαλακός.

Though I can provide no line of epic poetry which can have served as point of origin for this developemnt, I nonetheless feel that something like the following must have taken place. Originally there existed only the word δαμαλος, -η 'tame', but

beside it there later was created the word δάμαλις, a particularizing feminine used generally of cows. In the course of time
δάμαλις replaced δαμαλος to such an extent that the meaning of
the word was pretty much, if not entirely, forgotten. Thereupon a
poet, presented with a line similar to *Od.* 20.14 such as:

ὡς δαμάλῃσι κύων περὶ ἧς σκυλάκεσσι βεβῶσα

interpreted δαμαλῃσι as δ᾽ ἀμαλῃσι, took ἀμαλῃσι to be a
synonym of ἀπαλῇσι, and thus introduced into the epic vocabulary the word ἀμαλός, a word which was picked up by later
poets only occasionally, and which caused lexicographers great
difficulties. The abstraction of ἀμαλός sealed the doom of δαμαλος,
and it disappeared completely (save for the citation in Herodian).
There is no prothetic vowel in ἀμαλός, at least not in terms of the
definition of prothetic vowel given above, for there was no ἀμαλός
of IE origin.[17]

2.2.6 Schwyzer, comparing Skt. *mrjanti* 'sie wischen', and citing
also Grk. ἀμέργω (Sappho *PLF* 122, Eur. *HF* 397) 'pluck, pull'
and μόρξαντο, includes ὀμόργνυμι (*Il.* 5.416) 'wipe' among cases
of vocalic prothesis. And Frisk (2.389-390) agrees that the vowel
is prothetic, adding further the gloss: ὄμαρξον· ἀπόμαξον (Hsch.)
which he compares directly with Skt. *amrksat, amrksa*. And if
this etymological connection is correct, and there seems no good
reason to suppose that it is not, then we must assume a prothetic
vowel even though it goes against the rule: no prothesis before
/Ro/.

---

[17] The development I have sketched in the text is of course hypothetical,
and no amount of support will be able to convince the skeptical. Nonetheless I
do at least owe the reader a parallel or two, and offer *Odyssey*
17.471   ὁππότ᾽ ἀνὴρ περὶ οἷσι μαχειόμενος κτεάτεσσι
as a parallel for περὶ ἧς, and
20.25   ὡς δ᾽ ὅτε γαστέρ᾽ ἀνὴρ πολέος πυρὸς αἰθομένοιο
as a parallel for ὡς δ᾽. I cannot at present find any support for the somewhat
strained word order. Perhaps it is best simply to leave the explanation as
exempli gratia only, and not insist on it to the exclusion of other, perhaps
equally possible, explanations. I hope, though, that my formulation of the rules
governing prothesis — which excludes prothesis here — will prove sufficiently
compelling that no one will be tempted to admit prothesis in this word.

The question that then must be faced concerns the form
μόρξαντο without prothesis which occurs in Quintus Smyrnaeus:

4.269					ἐκ δὲ μετώπων

χερσὶν ἅδην μόρξαντο κατεσσύμενόν περ ἱδρῶτα

4.373					ἀπέπνευσαν καμάτοιο

μορξάμενοι σπόγγοισι πολυτρήτοισι μέτωπα

Does Quintus here preserve a genuine ancient tradition, or is this
simply another case of "analogical reduction" (Frisk 2.390 following Strömberg 1944:45); or are these artistically constructed
forms? The following is the textual evidence I have found for a
root *morg-. In *Il.* 5.798 Leaf's DHMRST read ἀπεμόργνυ for
ἀπομόργνυ; in *Il.* 2.269 all mss. save ACJT²U read ἀπεμόρξατο
for ἀπομόρξατο; in *Il.* 18.414 ACJPSfr.Mosc. read ἀπεμόργνυ for
ἀπομόργνυ. In *Il.* 18.124 one could read δάκρυα μορξαμένην for
δάκρυ ὁμορξαμένην; in *Od.* 8.88 δάκρυα μορξάμενος; in *Od.* 11.530
δάκρυα μορξάμενον, both for δάκρυ ὁμορξάμενος/ν. There would
then remain in the Homeric poems as secure evidence for ὁμοργ-,
Il. 5.416: ἀπ᾽ ἰχῶ χειρὸς ὁμόργνυ (we could de rigueur read
ἐμόργνυ even here) and *Od.* 11.527: δάκρυα τ᾽ ὠμόργνυντο, as well
as the attestation of the mss. at *Il.* 23.739 for ἀπομορξαμένω. I
cannot judge the mss. attestation at *Od.* 17.304: ἀπομόρξατο and
18.200: ἀπομόρξατο. A fair case can therefore be made for
Homeric μοργ- beside ὁμοργ-. But it unfortunately falls apart
when we consider that Homer's ὠμόργνυντο can stem only from
ὁμοργ-, and that Attic is entirely consistent in its ἀπομόργνυμι
perf. ἀπωμοργμένος (Arist. *Physiogn.* 6.6), and more importantly
ἐξομόργνυμι. Furthermore all cases of μοργ- attested in the
Homeric mss. occur in secondary tenses of ἀπομόργνυμι, and
surely represent the usual scribal uncertainty as to whether the
augment was or was not to be used wherever it was possible.
That ἀπεμοργ- is not the proper augmented form of ἀπομοργ-
would not have deterred later scribes who may have analyzed
ἀπομόργνυμι as a compound of ἀπό + μόργνυμι. And the
evidence for δάκρυα μορξάμενος was of course tendentiously
invented by me, and is therefore worthless: the Homeric form,
and the only Homeric form, of this root was ὁμοργ-. But it does

seem that in some texts or traditions the reading δάκρυα μορξάμενος must have existed, for otherwise Quintus' forms — notice that he uses this form only in the aorist, the tense in which the Homeric δάκρυ ὀμορξ- occurs — would be inexplicable. We may conclude that ὀμοργ- was the only form of this stem in use throughout the classical period, and that a form μοργ- without prothesis never existed as a normal form in historical Grk. dialects, though there were numerous phrases which could be so interpreted by poets.[18]

But having established this much simply makes the problem worse, for I have supposed above that prothesis does not occur before /o/. Here two considerations come into play: the first is Hesychius' gloss cited above: ὄμαρξον· ἀπόμαξον which, if not some sort of conflation with ἀπομάσσω, proves that the /a/ grade was once present in this root: we may thus suppose a stage *(ə)marks- or *(ə)marg- in the development of the aorist of this verb. The second is the generally accepted etymological connection of this verb with ἀμέργω 'pluck'. And though these two verbs are semantically somewhat distant, they are not sufficiently so to destroy the connection.[19] And if they are related, then *əmarg- must have derived from a still earlier *mrg- (cf. Skt. mrnákti — Frisk 2.390), and the o-vowel must then be secondary. We are therefore free to imagine that *amerg- ∾ *mrg- became *amerg- ∾ *amrg- through analogical extension of the /a/ (< ə)

---

[18] But we shall see below (6.2.2) that a case can yet be made for an aorist *marks- (and not *omarks-), for prothesis before syllables closed by /r/ occurs only when /r/ is followed by a voiced or aspirated consonant. It seems unlikely, though, that this is the explanation here.

[19] Though 'pluck' and 'wipe' are two different operations, the same organ, the hand, is used in both. Cf. Eur. HF 395:

χρυσέων πετάλων ἄπο μηλοφόρον χερὶ καρπὸν ἀμέρξων

and Il. 18.124:

ἀμφοτέρῃσιν χερσὶ παρειάων ἀπαλάων

δάκρυ᾽ ὀμορξαμένην ἀδινὸν στοναχῆσαι ἐφείην

The original meaning of these words may therefore have been something like 'remove with the hand'. If so, they may be further connected with μάρη 'hand' and Lat. manus, thus deriving from an IE root *mār, manós (Pok. 740-741 — Pok. writes mər-), and possibly also with μάρπτω 'take hold of'.

from the full-grade form to the zero-grade form. But perhaps a still more likely development can be represented and displayed as follows:

	present	aorist
1)	mrgnūmi	mrksa
2)	margnūmi	marksa
3)	amargnūmi	marksa
4)	amargnūmi	amarksa
5)	amorgnūmi	amarksa → amorksa
6)	omorgnūmi	omorksa

In this event the prothetic vowel will have developed, in accordance with the rule, before the closed syllable *marg-. And only later, after the -αρ- was assimilated by the following -υ- to -ορ- (cf. στόρνυμι θόρνυμι ὄλλυμι ὄμνυμι from στάρνυμι θάρνυμι, etc. Schmidt 1893: 376-390) did the initial ἀ- become rounded to ὀ- (as in ὄροφος < ἔροφος beside ἐρέφω). Clearly stages 1-4 of the development sketched above are now irretrievable, but possibly stage 5 can be inferred from Quintus' μόρξαντο. If any of the phrases containing δάκρυ ὀμοργ- were originated (and written) before initial ἀ- was replaced by ὀ-, clearly they would have appeared in mss. as ΔΑΚΡΥΑΜΟΡΞΑΝΤΟ. And since this arrangement corresponded to no words known in later times, one could infer either that δάκρυα μόρξαντο or δάκρυ ὀμόρξαντο was meant.[20]

2.2.7 We may therefore assume that prothesis in this case developed before the syllable *marg- (or was brought over from ἀμέργω), and may summarize the results with */m/ as follows. Again I express the rules in terms of the following vowel.

$$\text{i)} \qquad {}^*\text{me}\begin{bmatrix} i \\ l \end{bmatrix}\text{C-} \qquad \rightarrow \qquad {}^*\text{əme}\begin{bmatrix} i \\ l \end{bmatrix}\text{C-}$$

ἀμείβω ἀμέλγω ὀμείχω

---

[20] Stage 5) in the development sketched above is also supported by Hesychius' gloss: ἀμόρξαι· ἀποψῆσαι. ἢ ὀμόρξαι.

ii) $*\text{ma}\begin{bmatrix}\text{r}\\\text{l}\end{bmatrix}\text{C-}$ → $*\text{əma}\begin{bmatrix}\text{r}\\\text{l}\end{bmatrix}\text{C-}$

ἀμαλδύνω ἀμάργνυμι

iii) $*\text{mik}^{\text{h}}\text{l-}$ → $*\text{əmik}^{\text{h}}\text{l-}$

ὀμίχλη

And the same restriction on prothesis before */mo/ obtains as before */lo/. Thus, if we now extend the class resonant to include /l/, we may utilize the same rule we established above for initial */l/: initial */m/ followed by a non-rounded vowel in a syllable closed either by a resonant followed by a consonant, or a consonant followed by a resonant, develops a vocalic onset of uncertain color (prothetic vowel). Again schematically:

$$*\text{m}\begin{bmatrix}\text{e}\\\text{a}\\\text{i}\end{bmatrix}\begin{bmatrix}\text{RC}\\\text{CR}\end{bmatrix}\quad\rightarrow\quad *\text{əm}\begin{bmatrix}\text{e}\\\text{a}\\\text{i}\end{bmatrix}\begin{bmatrix}\text{RC}\\\text{CR}\end{bmatrix}$$

where again C stands for any consonant and R for the class of non-nasal semivowels and resonants.

2.3.0 Since the rule as just given works for */l/ and */m/, we now have every reason to suppose that it will operate before */n/ as well. Secure cases of prothesis are, however, rare before */n/, and in several cases at least do not conform readily to the rule given above. One reason for this, as we shall see, is that PIE */n/ was susceptible of vocalization under certain phonological conditions; and furthermore, it had a grammatical function as the unstressed variety of *ne 'not' and *en 'in' (Seiler 1957).

2.3.1 The only certain case of prothesis which conforms to my rules is ὄνειδος (Il. 1.291), 'reproach, rebuke', included by Lejeune, though not by Schwyzer. There are no other forms of this root in Greek and ὀνειδ- always serves as the base form, but there are numerous extra-Grk. cognates (Frisk 2.394) such as Skt. níndati 'blame' and Goth. ganaitjan 'revile' which show that the PIE root was *nid-. The immediately pre-Greek form was *neid- which, with prothesis, developed to *əneid- > *oneid-.

2.3.2 Lejeune includes ἀνεψιός 'first-cousin' (*Il.* 9.464), followed in this by Frisk (1.106), while Schwyzer (1939:433) prefers to analyze the word as ἀ-νεψιός, the individualizing masculine to the collective *ἀνεψιά 'der Gesamtheit der *nepōtēs*': *ἀνεψιά contained ἀ-copulativum, and ἀνεψιός originally meant 'einer aus der *ἀνεψιά'. Schwyzer's derivation, though most attractive, is semantically difficult: *aneptiā should mean 'those having (sharing) the same *nepōs', hence should refer rather to uncles or grandfathers: cf. ἄλοχος 'sharing the same bed', hence 'wife' and ἀδελφός 'sharing the same womb', hence 'brother'; and if a meaning 'Gesamtheit der *nepōtēs' was required, we would imagine that it would have been created simply by the addition of the *-ia* suffix: cf. φρήτηρ = ἀδελφός (Hsch.): φρατρία 'tribe, clan', originally 'brotherhood'. Furthermore, exact parallels to ἀνεψιός exist in OCS *netьjь* 'nephew' and Ave. *naptya-* 'off-spring' which prove that *neptios was an already PIE derivative, though they do not of course prove that Grk. inherited this *neptios.

Two ways of explaining the initial vowel in this word as prothesis remain open: we can either assume that prothesis developed as regularly in a syllable closed by a consonant followed by a semivowel, extending the rule only to include clusters: *neC(C)S- → *əneC(C)S-. Or we can adopt a more elaborate explanation which would involve assuming the sonantization of the */n/- (> /a/-) in the no longer attested Grk. *népō(t)s np(t)ós > *ánepos *aptós*, which paradigm, as a result of a blend with the thematic paradigm *neptiós *neptióio gave rise to *aneptiós *aneptióio.[21] That is to say, original PIE had the paradigm *népōts *np(t)ós which developed, as regularly, to *népōs *ap(t)ós in proto-Grk., a paradigm which was then leveled to *ánepōs *aneptós*. At this time the *-yo* derivative *neptiós *neptióio picked up the initial /a/- from *ánepōs, thus yielding ἀνεψιός, and this newer, more regular, form, having the same meaning as *ánepōs, caused *ánepōs to disappear. The difficulty with this explanation is that nowhere else in IE do we find the

---

[21] νέποδες 'children' *Od.* 4.404 (Frisk 2.307-308) may be the only survival of *nepōs in Grk., if indeed it is cognate (denied by Beekes 1969:105-106).

zero-grade of */ne/- in this word (unless we resurrect Skt. *ápatyam* 'offspring' as cognate, but cf. Mayrhofer *KEW* 1.37, 2.133); elsewhere we find the full-grade vocalism throughout the paradigm, and it is thus better, at least provisionally, to extend the rule given above to include consonant clusters and assume that *neptios > *əneptios.[22]

2.3.3 Though neither Schwyzer nor Lejeune mention the words, ἔνερθε(ν) (*Il.* 11.234) '(from) beneath' beside νέρθεν (*Il.* 7.212) together with Doric ἔνερθα, and ἐνέρτερος (*Il.* 5.898) 'lower' beside νέρτερος (Attic) and ἐνέρτατος (Emp. 35.3), they should at least be mentioned here. All are problematic, for we find forms with prothesis beside forms without in the same word, and the rules would seem to demand ἐνερ- alone.[23] And ἔνεροι (*Il.* 15.188) 'those below', which might be taken to be the positive of (ἐ)νέρτερος and the base of ἔνερθεν, always contains a prothetic vowel in a syllabic environment for which prothesis is not predicted by my rules. It seems that the only way to explain this situation is to assume that prothesis developed, as regularly, in one form and then spread analogically to the others. We shall see (below 6.3.3) that the cluster -/rt/- does not allow prothesis, while -/rtʰ/- does. Hence prothesis developed in ἔνερθεν from *nertʰen, as regularly, while *neroi and *nerteros remained without prothesis. Subsequently, however, prothesis was option-ally extended to these latter two forms and the longer forms appeared sporadically thereafter. Conversely the forms without prothesis reacted on ἔνερθεν to produce the poetic νέρθεν.[24]

2.3.4 The three other examples of prothesis before */n/-: ἀνήρ 'man' (S.L.), ὄνομα 'name' (neither S. nor L.), ἐννέα 'nine' (L.) all

---

[22] If, that is, we exclude ἀ-copulative. But analogy can save Schwyzer's explanation: *neptios > *əneptios after ἀδελφός and ἄλοχος.

[23] Or rather would allow, since I am here providing only the rules limiting the occurrence of prothesis to certain word shapes and have not maintained that prothesis always occurs under these conditions. But prothesis has thus far been seen to be consistent within a given word.

[24] There is also the relation κεῖθεν ~ ἐκεῖθεν which may well have influenced the creation of νέρθε.

constitute exceptions to my rule, but all, save ἐννέα, can be
explained by assuming that PIE */n/- became *[n̥] > Grk. /a/
(> /o/ before /u/). All recur with prothesis in Arm., and hence
ἀνήρ and ὄνομα at least are not of the same type of purely Grk.
prothesis as that so far discussed. But they do have a relatively
simple and straightforward explanation, and might profitably be
discussed here.[25]

The prothetic vowel in ἀνήρ is the result of a leveling of the
irregular paradigm */né:r/, */arós/ by extension of the /a/ (<
/n/) of the oblique cases to the nominative and accusative cases:
thereupon the stem of the word was taken to be /an/-, and this
/an/- was introduced to the oblique cases. The original PIE
paradigm of this word in the singular was (to treat those cases
preserved in Grk. as being the only PIE forms):

   /né:r/   /nrós/   /nrí/   /nérm/

From these there developed in Grk., after the vocalization of the
sonant resonants, the paradigm:

   /né:r/   /arós/   /arí/   /néra/

This irregular paradigm was leveled by introducing /a/ to the
nominative and accusative:

   /ané:r/   /arós/   /arí/   /anéra/

Thereupon /an/- formed the base of the paradigm and was
extended to the oblique cases, and the classical paradigm resulted:[26]

   /ané:r/   /andrós/   /andrí/   /anéra/

---

[25] The explanations of ἀνήρ and ὄνομα which follow appear also (in
modified form) in Wyatt 1969b:65-71. The explanation of ἀνήρ appears also in
Wyatt 1970:26.

[26] There are two possible objections to this formulation. The first holds
that initial *[n̥r] ought to pass, not to */ar/-, but to */anr/- (= */andr/-):
analogies here include βαίνω which is generally derived from *gʷmyo, and
which shows *[m̥] passing to /am/ before a resonant (semivowel). But of
course the environments are not the same in the first place, and one can easily
allege as counterexamples the numerous compounds of the negative prefix plus

2.3.5 Laryngealists have been quick to set up an initial laryngeal to account for the Grk. prothesis in ὄνομα, (Benveniste 1935:181), but they have been discouraged by Cowgill (1965:152), who points out that there is little evidence for a laryngeal in this word. Not only is there no lengthening of the first element in Vedic compounds with *nāma-*, but the Hitt. form *la-a-ma-an* is decidedly opposed to H_1enH_3- ∿ H_1neH_3-, for from such a form one would expect an initial *h*- or *a*- in Hitt. The following states of the root are attested:

*$\bar{n}\bar{o}mn̥$:   Lat. *nōmen*, Skt. *nāma*

*$nomn̥̥$:   Umb. *nome*, Grk. ὄνομα, Goth. *namo*

*$n̥mn̥-$:   OIr. *ainm*, OCS *imę*

The lengthened vowel of *nōmen* has been plausibly explained by Cowgill (1965:156) as a conflation of *nomen* with the root *gnō- 'to know'. He also attributes the long *ā* of Skt. *nāma* to the action of Brugmann's Law. With the lengthened-grade forms no longer a problem only two grades of the root remain: */nómn/ and */nmn-/ (Szemerényi 1964:243-245). Clearly they represent the strong form and the weak form respectively of an original paradigm: */nómn/, gen. */nmnós/, in Grk. *nóma, *amnós.[27]

/l m n/ such as ἀληθής ἀμελής ἄνομος. Furthermore assuming *[n̥] > /an/ /__[r̥] destroys once and for all any possibility of explaining the anomalous scansion of ἀνδρότητα (= [arotɛːta]?) in *Il.* 16.857 = 22.363, 24.6.

A more serious objection involves the Hesychian gloss δρώψ· ἄνθρωπος and the assumption that [nr]- > [dr]- in Grk., a development supposed to be parallel to *[ml]- > [bl]- in βλώσκω (< *[mlɔ:]-) and *[mr]- > [br]- in βροτός (< *[mr̥tós]). About these latter developments there is reason to doubt: βλώσκω is probably taken from the perfect μέμβλωκα (cf. θνήσκω τέθνηκα) and *[mrtos], because the [r̥] was sonant, could not develop [m̥]: the chances are that *mr̥tós > *mrotós > brotós considerably later than the changes involving [n̥] and [m̥]. And what is more, δρώψ is almost certainly a grammarian's invention (cf. Frisk 1.422). Hence I feel that there is no reason to question a rule: initial [n̥] > /a/ /__[r].

[27] One might object to this formulation that */nmnós/, containing as it does three semivowels (resonants) in a row should, in accord with

In Greek of course all -*n*- stems received a -*t*- extension in the oblique cases such that the vocalism of the nominative was carried through the entire paradigm. But we must imagine that this development took place after the vocalization of initial *[ņ] and after the resulting */a/ had been extended to the nominative: hence *nóma *amnós → *ánoma *amnós → *ánoma *anómatos. Then, with the raising of /o/ normal before labialization in Grk. (as in νύξ < *nok^ws, ὄνυξ < *anok^wh, — Szemerényi 1964:240, Cowgill 1965:156-157), there arose *anuma *anumatos, which in turn because of the again normal assimilation of /a/ to /o/ before /u/ (Schmidt 1893:376-390) passed to *onuma *onumatos. Attic has either preserved the original quality of the vowel in some environment, or has experienced still another assimilation which led to ὄνομα ὀνόματος. Hence, in schematic form:[28]

I	*/nomn/	>	*/noma/
	*/nmnos/	>	*/amnos/
II	*/noma/	→	*/anoma/
	*/amnos/	→	*/anomatos/
III	*/anoma/	>	*/anuma/
	*/anomatos/	>	*/anumatos/
IV	*/anuma/	>	ὄνυμα
	*/anumatos/	>	ὀνύματος

Sievers-Edgerton rules, develop to *nanós, and not to *amnós. But surely this is to show an excess of zeal for formalism and a disregard for phonetic likelihood. Sonant [m̥] and [ņ] do not develop from consonantal [m] and [n] as is sometimes held, but rather from syllabic [m̥] and [ņ], i.e., syllable peaks which replace earlier syllables containing a vowel. Hence it might be better in order to avoid misunderstandings, to present developments as follows: *nomnós > *n^omnós > *ņmnós > *amnós. In this way we can indicate that the initial syllable always remained a syllable regardless of what the nucleus of that syllable was. Similarly with *ner: *nerós > *n^erós > *ņrós > *aros, and with βαίνω: *g^wemyṓ > *g^{we}myṓ > *g^wm̥yṓ > *g^wā́yō > *g^wányō.

[28] ὄνυξ beside Skt. nakha-, Russ. noga seems to be a case almost precisely similar to that of ὄνομα. The IE root must have had the two forms *nóghs and *nghós (Szemerényi 1964:240), and these words yielded *nóks akhós in Grk. This irregular paradigm in turn gave rise to a nominative *anoks > *anuks > ὄνυξ, and this last formed the basis for the entire paradigm.

V   ὄνυμα   >   ὄνομα in Attic-Ionic
     ὀνύματος   >   ὀνόματος

2.3.6 ἐννέα 'nine', ἔνατος 'ninth' together with all its derivatives (forms assembled by Szemerényi 1964:107) causes real problems. All other IE languages save Armenian point to an original *newn̥, and the Grk. ἐ- is therefore not a feature inherited from PIE. It has become traditional by now to equate Grk. ἐννέα and Arm. inn and to postulate a common origin for the prothesis, thus assuming an Armeno-Hellenic */e/- of prothetic origin (like ἔρεβος 'Erebos', Arm. erek 'evening') and hence a common form *enewn̥ (Frisk 1.519-520). But as Szemerényi (1964:112) points out, since Grk. and Arm. do not always agree in their prothetic forms, there is no real need to assume common origin here. Szemerényi further believes that ἔνατος < *enwatos derives from earlier *enewatos by syncope, and, since ἐννέα has an unoriginal geminate, that all Grk. forms derive from a proto-Grk. *enewa directly derivable from PIE *newn̥.

The origin of the syllable ἐν- in ἐννέα is difficult, and I would be willing to accept initial [n̥] > /a/ (as in ἀνήρ and ὄνομα) > /e/ if I could find some way of providing a phonological motivation for this change; or to assume the analogical pressure of ἑπτά ὀκτώ *νέϝα > *ἐνέϝα > ἐννέϝα, a development favored by some, but dismissed by Szemerényi (1964:111-112). But since the three initial sounds of the PIE form, */neu/, are among those sounds that under certain circumstances produce a prothetic vowel; and since a prothetic vowel does develop in Greek, *əneu-, I prefer to assume that somehow *neu- was placed in an environment in which prothesis could develop. I therefore feel that prothesis in ἐννέα (unlike that in ἀνήρ and ὄνομα) is subject to the rules of prothesis already established.

Finding the environment will be more difficult, and I have no great faith that the succession of developments I am about to produce is actually correct, though I am reasonably sure that something similar actually did take place. The IE numerals are so remarkably complex in their various developments and mutual influences (Szemerényi 1960) that almost anything seems possible, and the Grk. numbers involving 'nine' are definitely remodeled. To begin with what is not controversial, the cardinal numbers from seven to ten in IE, Skt., Lat. and Grk. were as follows:

	IE	Skt.	Lat.	Grk.
7.	*septm	sapta	septem	ἑπτά
8.	*oktō(u)	aṣṭau	octō	ὀκτώ
9.	*neun[29]	nava	novem	ἐννέα
10.	*dekmt	daśa	decem	δέκα

Only slightly more controversial is the assumption that the ordinal numerals in PIE were formed originally by merely adding the thematic vowel -/o/- to the cardinals (Szemerényi 1960:70), thus yielding (in my phonemic writing) the numerals: */septmos/ */oktowos/ */neunos/ */dekmtos/. These forms suffered or experienced numerous minor changes in the daughter languages, but it is clear enough that all can be recognized, slightly modified, in the daughter languages, including Lat. *nōnus* (< *nowenos* remodeled from *neunos* > *nūnus* after *novem*):

	IE	Skt.	Lat.	Grk.
7.	*septmos	saptama	septimus	ἕβδομος
8.	*oktowos	aṣṭama	octāvus	ὄγδοος
9.	*neunos	navama	nōnus	ἔνατος
10.	*dekmtos	daśama	decimus	δέκατος

Only Grk., which seems to require an earlier *enwatos*, diverges greatly. It is clear that a proto-Grk. *neunos* would develop to *əneunos*, and it seems altogether simplest to assume that in Grk. this *neunos* > *əneunos* once existed, but that beside it there also existed a *newatos* influenced by *dekatos* (Szemerényi 1960: 89,93): final -/t/ was lost early on in Grk., and as a result the relation *deka* — *dekatos* was felt to be numeral plus -*tos*, and

---

[29] *newn̥ is usually written, but in PIE [n̥] was merely the vocalic allophone of /n/, or so it is usually said. Hence if prothesis developed early enough, that is to say within the Hellenic dialect of PIE, it might be possible to assume that *neun > *əneun > *ənewa, and the more complicated developments presented below avoided. But this explanation would fail to account for the double nasal in ἐννέα, and prothesis cannot have been this early.

this feeling gave rise to *newatos beside *əneunos. These two forms (and as we shall suppose below, *əneunatos) must have coexisted for some time until *newatos (with the prothetic vowel picked up from *əneunos, and hence now *ənewatos) replaced *əneunos (and *əneunatos) because better supported by the system of ordinals, and particularly by *dekatos.[30]

When we consider the decads, a similar picture emerges. It is tolerably clear that the decads were formed by adding *dkont to the cardinals (Szemerényi 1960:135-136), a formative which is no longer completely visible, for the */d/ appears typically as length of the preceding vowel. And 70-90 in PIE must have therefore been */septm:kont/ */okto:kont/ */newn:knot/. These forms gave in Grk. *septmākont(a) *oktōkont(a) *əneunākont(a) (Szemerényi 1964:114) which of course finally became ἑβδομήκοντα ὀγδοήκοντα, both under the influence of the ordinal, and *eneunēkonta > *enenēkonta with simplification of the diphthong -eu- > -e- because -u- now appeared nowhere else in the paradigm of 'nine'.

Thus both 'ninth' and 'ninety' have a prothetic vowel by perfectly regular, though complicated, means. The question of 'nine' itself, ἐννέα, is more difficult. It does not seem possible that *newa would pass directly to *enewa because the /w/ is not in the same syllable as the /e/: the prothetic vowel must therefore be analogical to 'ninth' or 'ninety'. Just how is hard to say, but since ἐννέα differs from the PIE form both by virtue of the prothetic vowel and of the double nasal, I shall assume that PIE (PGrk.) *newa > *en-newa directly because prefixed by en-. This en- could have been most any en-, but was most likely the en- of en-enēkonta taken to be some sort of prefix, and hence prefixed directly to *newa. This supposition can be supported by certain facts of the historically attested numeral forms. If we look at the numbers for '90' found in Grk., we see that beside ἐνενήκοντα, the

---

[30] On this theory, which follows Szemerényi 1964:115, *ἐνέϝατος experienced syncope to *ἔνϝατος. I shall offer another, more complicated, explanation below which will not require the assumption of syncope.

most usual form, there occur also ἐννήκοντα (*Od.* 19.174), clearly an analogical creation to ἐννέα, and ἐνήκοντα (IG 11(2).199 B 32 — Delos, 3rd c.), equally clearly an abbreviated form of ἐνενήκοντα, a form minus ἐν-, which shows that the ἐν- was separable, or could be so regarded. I presume that the ἐν- of ἐνενήκοντα was extended also to *newa, thus giving ultimately ἐννέα.[31]

---

[31] The development sketched in the text is designed simply to account for the prothetic vowel in ἐννέα, and is certainly not designed finally to settle the relations of */ennewa/ */enwatos/ (?) */*enenēkonta*/. Perhaps here it would be well to give a schematic representation of what I feel *may* have happened.

PIE	*neun	*neunos	*neun:kont
		*neunatos (1)	
PGrk. I	*newa	*əneunatos	*əneunēkonta
PGrk. II	*ən-newa (2)	*ən-eunatos	*ən-enēkonta (3)
		*eunatos (4)	*enēkonta (4)
	*ēnatos (5)	*enatos (6)	
Class.	ἐννέα	εἴνατος	ἔνατος ἐνενήκοντα ἐνήκοντα

(1) *neunatos after *dekatos.
(2) *ənnewa with **ən-* from 'ninth' and '90'.
(3) *əneunēkonta > *ənenēkonta by simplification of the diphthong.
(4) With **en-* regarded as a separable prefix — the counterpart of (2).
(5) *-*eu*- > *-*ē*- necessary because of the argument. If we could assume a PGrk. *enenewatos > *enenwatos > *enwatos (> *ēnatos), we could avoid metaphysics here
(6) directly after *dekatos.

The first reader of this work has suggested an alternative to the assumption that *en- was analogically extended in toto from 'ninth' and '90'. He has in his own dialect of English (in his transcription) /e:t´ti:n/ '18' with doubled *t*, and this doubled *t* has led analogically to a doubled *t* in '19' (= /naynt´ti:n/) where it does not legitimately belong. He feels that the analogy of 'seven' and 'eight' in Grk., both with closed first syllables followed by an accented syllable, played a part in developing ἐννέα. This seems to me plausible, and we might then assume that *néwa > *ənéwa > *enéwa (with the *ə from 'ninth' and '90') > *ennéwa (with the resonant doubled analogically after 'seven' and 'eight').

2.3.7 Thus only four examples of Grk. prothesis before */n/ remain, ὄνειδος ἐννέα ἀνεψιός ἔνερθε, only the first two of which are really secure, but all fit the scheme I have given above. We may thus state (provisionally, for we may yet need to restrict or extend things) that prothesis occurs before */l m n/ only when they are followed by a non-rounded vowel in a heavy syllable closed either by a (non-nasal) resonant plus consonant or by a consonant plus (non-nasal) resonant.

2.4.0 The same rule applies, with only minor modifications required, before */w/ as well, as a glance at the secure examples will show, though here things are less certain since the prothetic vowel seems in general to have disappeared together with the */w/. I shall treat first those words accepted by both Schwyzer and Lejeune.

2.4.1 ἔεδνα (*Od.* 1.277) 'wedding gifts' beside ἕδνα (*Il.* 16.178). This word is always included among cases of prothesis alternating with non-prothetic forms, but there is some likelihood that the forms without prothesis are mirages. ἕδνα occurs seven times in Homer, while all other forms and derivatives show ἐε-: ἔεδνα (4x), ἐέδνωταί (*Il.* 13.382), ἐέδνοισι (3x), ἐεδνώσαιτο (*Od.* 2.53), ἀνάεδνον (*Il.* 9.146). Furthermore, ἕδνα, save for two occurrences after καί (*Od.* 11.117, 13.378) for which we can easily substitute ἔεδνα, occurs only in the phrases ἀπερείσια ἕδνα (*Il.* 16.178, *Od.* 19.529) and μυρία ἕδνα (*Il.* 16.190, 22.472, *Od.* 11.282), phrases reminiscent of the only other occurrence of ἀπερείσιος, the frequent ἀπερείσι' ἄποινα. ἔεδνα occurs only after *nu*-movable, a position in which it cannot be changed to ἕδνα. But of course ἀπερείσια ἕδνα can easily, on the model of ἀπερείσι' ἄποινα, be changed to ἀπερείσι' ἄεδνα. I feel that this is in fact the correct original form of the phrase, and that all later forms without prothesis are derived from this one phrase. ἀπερείσι' ἄεδνα was falsely reanalyzed as ἀπερείσια ἕδνα and ἕδνα taken over into the later poetic language (so Beekes 1969:58-59). All other cases of ἄεδνα in the poems then passed to ἔεδνα, an accommodation to the supposed colloquial ἕδνα.[32] I do not know where the aspiration in this new ἕδνα came from, but suppose that ancient poets felt that the allomorph ἀ- of the negative prefix ἀν- implied aspiration in the base form, as in the case of ἀεκών derived from ἑκών,[33] or Sommer (1905:103-104) could be right in adopting the ancients' suggestion of analogical influence of ἥδω.

2.4.2 εἴκοσι (Att.-Ion.) ἐείκοσι (for *ewīkosi — Il. 9.123) beside Doric ϝίκατι 'twenty' < *wīkati < *wīkṇti (Frisk 1.453-454). Prothesis seems not to have developed in the Doric dialects in this case and in most others.

2.4.3 ἐέργω (Il. 2.617), Attic εἴργω (εἵργω) beside ἔργω ἔργνυμι (Il. 17.571, Od. 10.238) 'bar the way' < *werg- (Frisk 1.465-

[32] Indeed it seems that the prothetic vowel before */we-/ was always ἀ-, and not ἐ-. This fact is indicated not only by Cretan ἄερσαν (2.4.5) and Hesiodic ἀνάελπτος (2.4.7), but also by ἀείδω (3.4.2) and ἄησι (4.4.3), forms which preserved the prothetic vowel. But when prothesis was lost, only during the period of oral epic composition, apparently, certain verses in the Hom. poems were deficient one mora, a deficiency then made up by lengthening the initial vowel of the word normal in prose. Thus ἐέλδωρ was pronounced [ēldɔ̄r] with the [ē] slurred over two syllables, and not as [e'eldɔ̄r] (or something) with a glottal catch separating two individually articulated epsilons. In this, then, the tendency was exactly the same as with diektasis: ὁράασθαι (Od. 16.107) was metrically ‒ ‒ ‒ > , but phonetically [horāsthai]. The same explanation accounts, incidentally, for Herodotean spellings like ἐποίεε which are to be understood as representing [epoiē], not [epoie'e].

[33] It will turn out later, though, that if we assume prothesis in this word (*wedna > *əwedna > ἄεδνα), it will be the only case of prothesis developing before *we- followed by a voiced stop. It will therefore be isolated, and prothesis as an explanation then becomes questionable. Perhaps we can follow Hesychius' lead, or rather his uncertainty, and assume that ἄεδνον means πολύφερνον, and is therefore a copulative compound with ἀ-copulative, (cf. Frisk 1.1, Chantraine 1968.2). This assumption will help also to explain the Iliad's strange ἀνάεδνον: it can now be seen to be the negativized form of the copulative compound. The word is usually connected with Lith. vedù and OCS vedǫ 'lead' (Frisk 1.442-443), and ἄεδνα will have originally been a participle meaning 'things brought along' or 'things accompanying the leading home'. ἄεδνα (or ἔεδνα) is a case of false prothesis and no longer to be included among secure cases of prothesis.

466).[34] Prothesis never occurs in the aorist while aspiration does
(ἐφέρξοντι συνhέρξοντι Schwyzer 1923:62.131,133 — Heraclea 4th
c.), a fact which caused Beekes (1969:62-63) to assume two stems
*$H_1\underset{.}{u}erg$- and *serg-. This latter is unnecessary as we shall see
below (6.3.3).

2.4.4 ἐέλδομαι (Il. 7.4) beside ἔλδομαι (Il. 5.481) 'wish for', ἐέλδωρ
(epic only) 'wish' < *weld- (Frisk 1.485).

2.4.5 ἐέρση (Il. 11.53), ἔερσα (Pi. N. 3.67), ἄερσαν· τὴν δρόσον.
Κρῆτες (Hsch.), ἀέρσην (PLit.Lond. 60) 'dew' beside ἔρσαι (Od.
9.222) 'kids', ἐερσήεις (Il. 24.419) beside ἐρσήεις (Il. 24.757)
'dewy' < *wers- (Frisk 1.566-567). The Homeric forms again
show the assimilation of ἀε- > ἐε- after the prose form, if indeed
ἔρση is a legitimate prose form.

2.4.6 ἐίση, always in the feminine (Il. 1.468), 'equal, fair', beside
ἶσος (Il. 1.187) 'equal' < *wītswos ? (Frisk 1.737-738). Schwyzer
cites this example, but elsewhere in his work (1939:104), and not
in his discussion of prothesis. Beekes (1969:65-66) concludes that
ἐίση arose from misdivision of the phrase πάντοσεϝίσην. This
seems most unlikely. For more on this word cf. n. 36 below.

2.4.7 The above, save for ἔεδνα, may be considered sure cases of
prothesis, and can serve as a basis for further discussion. They
have in common */we/ followed by r/lCons. except for εἴκοσι and
ἐίση where the prothetic vowel developed before */wi:/ (=
/wiy/?) and */wi/. A number of other cases conform to these
requirements, but for one reason or another were not included by
Lejeune. Lejeune does, however, mention one example not cited

[34] It is unlikely that Attic εἴργω directly continues ἐέργω, and rather more
likely that somehow ἔργω was replaced by εἴργω in Attic. There are numerous
reasons for this assumption. 1) Ionic has but few εἰρ- forms, and normally
shows ἐργ-. 2) Attic is uncertain, and though εἰργ- is perhaps more frequent in
the verb, the noun ἔργμα 'fence' always has the shorter form. 3) is perhaps
only a sub-category of 1): if we assume prothesis in Attic here, this will be the
only case in which Attic has preserved the Homeric prothesis where Ionic has
not. 4) If Attic were to have kept the prothesis, we would expect ἀ- rather
than ἐ- (above n.32). For all these reasons I feel that, though I do not know
how to account for the form otherwise, εἴργω is not a development of earlier
ἐέργω. εἴργουσι (Il. 23.72) might be.

by Schwyzer. ἐέλπομαι (*Il.* 8.196) beside ἔλπομαι (*Il.* 3.112) 'hope, expect ' ἀνάελπτος (Hes. *Th.* 660) 'unlooked for' < *welp- (Frisk 1.502-503). Clearly this word is from the same root as ἐέλδομαι, and Schwyzer can have had no theoretical reason for not including it.

2.4.8 Now those cases of prothesis included only by Schwyzer: ἐέλσαι (*Il.* 21.295) beside the more common ἔλσαι (*Il.* 1.409, 18.294, 21.225) to Homeric εἴλομαι (*Il.* 5.782), Homeric (*Il.* 2.294) and Attic εἰλέω 'shut in, press', all from a root *wel- seen in various Slavic forms (Frisk 1.456-457), unless it is the same root *wel- 'turn' seen in εἰλέω ἴλλω 'wind' and εἰλύω 'enfold, enwrap' and hence cognate with Lat. *volvo* 'roll'. Prothesis occurs only in the one Homeric form ἐέλσαι (and possibly in ἐείλεον *Il.* 18.447). But to this ἐέλσαι the augmented aorist was *ēwelsamēn, the uncontracted form which lay behind ἠλσάμην (Semon. 17). Once the contraction had taken place, this word fell into the class of ε-initial verbs, and the analogy of ἐλπίσαι — ἤλπισα operated to create the newer ἔλσαι, which form then became the regular aorist. Beekes (1969:62), however, feels that ἐέλσαι is an artificial form.

2.4.9 εἴλη (or εἵλη) 'sun's warmth' beside ἔλη (Eust. 667.22, 1573.45), βέλα· ἥλιος, καὶ αὐγὴ ὑπὸ Λακώνων (Hsch.), γέλαν· αὐγὴν ἡλίου, γελοδυτία· ἡλιοδυσία; and εἰληθερής, εἰληθερέω (Hp. Gal.) 'warmed by the sun' beside ἐλαθερές· ἡλιοθαλπές (Hsch.); and εἰλόπεδον (perhaps, if the correct interpretation of mss. θειλόπεδον: Leumann 1950:44) 'sunny spot', πρόσειλος, εὔειλος (Attic drama) 'sunny', ἄειλος (A. *Fr.* 334) 'sunless'. Frisk (1.458-459) connects these words with Germanic and Baltic verbs meaning 'burn slowly, singe': OE *swelan*, Germ. *schwelen*, Lith. *svìlti*. The PIE form from which the Grk. words derived was *swelā > PGk. *hwelā which then gave Ϝελᾱ, ἔλᾱ, and with prothetic vowel, εἴλη, εἵλη < *ehwelā. He further connects ἀλέα 'warmth, heat, warm spot'. The difficulty here is that one would not expect prothesis before */hw/ in the first place (1.1.1 above), and secondly, if it were to occur beside non-prothetic forms, one would expect the relation ἐέλη > εἴλη : ἔλη (cf. ἔεδνα : ἔδνα), and not εἴλη : ἔλη. Of course analogy with ἥλιος or possibly leveling of the two variants εἴλη and ἕλη could account for the Attic rough breathing. But what is worse (from my point of view) is that prothesis should not occur at all before an open syllable *(h)wel-. I have no good explanation for these forms, but cannot, for the reasons just given, agree with Schwyzer that prothesis is involved.[35]

2.4.10 Ionic εἱλίσσω (εἰλίσσω) 'turn around or about' beside Homeric ἑλίσσω (*Il.* 1.317) and Attic ἑλίττω, ἕλιξ 'twisted, twist', ἑλιγμός 'winding', ἑλίκη 'winding'. But since only later Ionic, and neither Homer nor Attic, shows evidence of prothesis, we may assume that Ionic εἱλ- is a secondary development of ἑλ-, possibly on the basis of εἱλέω (Frisk 1.495-496). This verb at least cannot be included among the cases of prothesis.

2.4.11 An almost precisely similar situation exists with ἐρύω 'drag, draw'. Homer knows only the stem-form ἐρυ- (e.g. ἐρύοντα *Il.* 4.467), and the only early example of εἰρ- is Hesiod's εἰρύμεναι (*E.* 818). For the rest εἰρ- is known from Herodotus and Hippocrates: εἰρύσω (Hp. *Morb.* 2.8), εἰρύσαι (Hp. *Morb.* 1.29), εἰρύσας (Hdt. 4.10), εἰρυσάμενος (Hdt. 4.8). Hence, though Frisk (1.571) is willing to admit prothesis in this verb, I am not, and ascribe Ionic εἰρ- to the same tendency, whatever it was, which created εἱλίσσω.

2.4.12 To the list of prothetic forms can definitely be added the two words εἴδομαι, though Beekes (1969:59-60) denies prothesis, and οἴγνυμι. εἴδομαι 'seem, appear', together with εἶδος 'appearance' from which it is apparently derived, generally appears as such, but Homer also has the participial form ἐεισάμενος (*Il.* 2.22) and ἐεισαμένη (*Il.* 2.795) with prothesis. The word is clearly connected with the widespread root *wid- seen in Grk. εἶδον 'I saw' and οἶδα 'I know' (Frisk 1.451). Prothesis occurs before

---

[35] It is possible that the attested forms represent a conflation of the two derivatives of *swel-: *swelyā and *swelā. *swelyā would clearly develop to *hellā generally, but might also develop to *hēlā (cf. ἀείλη beside ἄελλα), while *swelā would clearly give *helā. Then, with the spread of the long vowel -ā to *hēlā, there would result *hēlā = εἵλη of which εἴλη is the psilotic form.

*weits- (*weiss-) but not before *wid- or *woid-.

2.4.13 οἴγνυμι 'open' is more difficult, but nonetheless the various forms attested do in fact seem to argue for a root *weig- which with prothesis developed to *oweig- > *oig- (Frisk 2.356-357). The forms which seem to require this analysis are the Aeolic infinitive ὀείγην (IG 12(2).6.43), and the participial ὀείγων (PLF Inc. Fr. 20). And if one takes these forms as a starting-point, one can easily restore to Homer numerous other examples of ὀειγ-. Thus, for ἀναοίγεσκον (Il. 24.455) can be restored ἀνοείγεσκον, and for ἀνέῳξε (Od. 10.389), ἀνέῳγε (Il. 16.221, etc.) *ἀνόειξε and *ἀνόειγε. Perhaps we are not justified in emending Homer in this way, but we are justified in assuming that οἴγω, οἴγνυμι is the contraction product of *oweig- with prothetic vowel to a root *weig-. The o-color of the prothetic vowel seems conditioned by the following i-diphthong: cf. ὀλ(ε)ίζων (2.1.7) and ὀμείχω (2.2.3) above. If genuine, and not falsely abstracted from the Homeric ὠΐγνυντο (Il. 2.809), the Hesychian ἴγνυντο· ἠνοίγοντο shows that prothesis did not develop before *wig.

2.4.14 Thus we find that prothesis before */w/ occurs only when that */w/ is followed by a front vowel /i:/ (= /iy/)[36] or /e/ (*/wa/ > */əwa/ is unexampled just as was */na/ > */əna/), and only when that front vowel is followed by /i l r/ in a closed

---

[36] It might be possible to avoid assuming /i:/, if we could regard the occasionally occurring ει forms for 'twenty' as in any way original. The Heraclean tables have ϝείκατι alternating with ϝίκατι, and Hsch. attributes a βείκατι to Laconian. But the Heraclean forms are probably influenced by Attic-Ionic εἴκοσι (Szemerényi 1960:23), and βείκατι is probably merely an itacistic spelling.

εἴση(ς) generally so spelled (and not *εἴσση) is possibly only secondarily attracted to ἴσος ἴση, and may quite possibly be for *ἐείση. In Homer the word modifies: νηῦς ἵππος ἀσπίς δαίς φρένες, and in all these cases (save Il. 2.765 where it compares two mares) the word could mean 'goodly' or 'seemly'. Hence it could be somehow connected with *weid- and (possibly) derive from *weidsa; or, if we can depart still farther from the attested forms and assume *ἐείσση, the word might be connected with the root *weik- seen in εἰκάζω and ἐπιεικής. On this reasoning the nominative *eweikyā must have been reformed (from *eweikyā) after the genitive *eweikyās. Speculations of this nature are not new: cf. Leaf's note to Il. 1.306.

syllable. Hence the restrictions on the development of prothesis are tighter in the case of */w/ than they are with any other resonant. But the problems are nonetheless greater. With every other resonant we have seen that prothesis is either constant in a word (save for (ἔ)νερθε(ν) — 2.3.3), or is predictable in terms of the different phonological shapes which that word assumes, as with λάχεια — ἐλάσσων (2.1.5). But no such possibility exists with */w/, for one and the same form of a given word appears both with prothesis and without, as in ἔλδομαι ἐέλδομαι (2.4.4). Furthermore, when prothesis does not occur, the initial vowel may either be aspirated (ἔρση) or unaspirated (ἔλδομαι). This particular problem, however, need not concern us here, for only with ἔργω εἴργω do we find both aspirated and unaspirated forms side by side, and we may therefore conclude that the major distinction was between forms with prothesis and those without: whether the form without prothesis was aspirated or not was a secondary problem, one to which we shall return below.

To speak in general terms the non-occurrence of prothesis before */w/ is not very difficult to explain. In the first place its effects will have been destroyed in the case of *Vwei-* by contraction: earlier *oweig-* develops to later *oig-* (οἴγω), and *ewei-* passes to *ei-* (εἶδος ?) in those cases (if there were any — above, n. 32) in which the prothetic vowel was *e-* and not *a-*. In the case of *ewe-* the long closed vowel may well have been shortened in a closed syllable: *ewe-* > *ee* > *ẹ̄* > *e/__CC*. Finally a number of instances cited above occurred in verbs in which prothesis and augment would have been homophonous, a homophony set aside by the removal of the "augment" from primary tenses, and perhaps most important from the non-indicative forms of the aorist. Thus *ἔελσα : ἐέλσαι* was very likely leveled out to *ἔελσα (beside *ἤελσα) : ἔλσαι. And so with other verbs. To be sure, ἔρση and ἴσος remain problematic, but not sufficiently so to cause undue difficulty to my rules which, it must be recalled, predict only the conditions under which prothesis occurs, not those under which it does not.

2.5 We can sum up the findings in this section statistically by saying that prothesis occurs as supposed (1.1.3) only in the following situations (26 cases):

$$R_1 V \begin{bmatrix} R_2 C_1 \text{-} \\ C_2 R_3 \end{bmatrix} \rightarrow \partial R V \begin{bmatrix} RC \\ CR \end{bmatrix}\text{-}$$

$R_1 \rightarrow$	/l/ 7x		$V \rightarrow$	/e/ 18x	
	/m/ 6x			/a/ 4x	
	/n/ 4x			/i/ 4x	
	/w/ 9x				

$R_2 \rightarrow$ /y/ 11x (where /y/ = [y] and [:] / /i/__)
 /w/ 2x
 /r/ 4x
 /l/ 5x

$C_1 \rightarrow$	/p/ 1x	/b/ 1x	/p^h/ 1x	/dz/ 1x	/n/ 2x
	/t/ 1x	/d/ 3x	/t^h/ 2x	/ts/ 2x	
	/k/ 1x	/g/ 4x	/k^h/ 1x	/s/ 2x	

$C_2 >$	/p^h/ 1x	/pt/ 1x		/k^h/ 2x
$R_3 >$	/y/ 2x	/r/ 1x	/l/ 1x	

These figures may later turn out to be significant, but at present the only fact that seems important is that *ReRC-* is the most frequent environment in which prothesis develops.

POSSIBLE ADDITIONAL CASES

3.0 With this formulation and these statistical facts in mind we can now treat other words which can be or have been included among cases of prothesis. The following fit the above rule, and hence are not phonologically excluded from the ranks of prothesis, though they may be for other reasons.

3.1.1 ἄλεισον (*Il.* 11.774) 'cup, goblet' if from *leitwon* (Schulze 1966:358-359 = *KZ* 29.255) and connected with Goth. *leipu* 'Obstwein', OHG *lid* 'geistiges Getränk'; or, since pouring is involved in the first mention of this word in the *Iliad* (11.774-775)

$$\text{ἔχε δὲ χρύσειον ἄλεισον}$$
$$\text{σπένδων αἴθοπα οἶνον ἐπ' αἰθομένοις ἱεροῖσιν}$$

with Russ. *liti* 'to pour' (Pok. 664-665). But Frisk has the odds on his side when he says of Schulze's suggestion: "Eher Mittelmeerwort" (1.67).

3.1.2 ἀλέξω (*Il.* etc.) 'ward off' beside Skt. *rakṣati* 'protects' could be included, but if it is, ἀλκή 'strength' would have to be considered a secondary formation (so Antilla 1969:175) created on the analogy of the relation ἀλέγω : ἄλγος, *ἀνέθω (cf. ἀνήνοθα): ἄνθος, in which event we should expect rather *ἄλκος. And since Skt. initial /a/ when unaccented disappears at least before a resonant (Wyatt 1970:26-28), it is perhaps best to assume a disyllabic *alek- as the IE root of these words (Cf. Frisk 1.68-70). Or we might prefer to assume a development like the following: *lek- → *lekseti, *lek → leká̄ > lká̄ > *alká̄ whereupon *leksei → aléksei. Prothesis, at least as usually conceived, seems not to be present in this root.

3.1.3 ἀλίγκιος (*Il.* 7.401, *Od.* 8.174) 'resembling, like' beside the more common ἐναλίγκιος, if connected with OCS *lice* 'face', could show prothesis, or could derive from *nlinkios < *enlinkios (Seiler 1957:16). But the connection with *lice* is far from certain (Frisk 1.73), and the relation between ἐναλίγκιος and ἀλίγκιος is obscure, with the rare ἀλίγκιος possibly a false abstraction from the longer form. If prothesis is involved, we shall have to extend *R* to include /n/.

3.1.4 ἀλινδέω (Nic. *Th.* 156) 'cause to roll' likewise could be included, but the word is late, obviously influenced by κυλινδέω, probably connected with εἰλέω, and hence from *wal- (Frisk 1.73). The /a/ is not prothetic.

3.1.5 ἐλαύνω (*Il.* 1.575) beside ἐλάω (*Il.* 5.366) 'drive' would fit, but almost certainly contains a disyllabic root *ela- (Frisk 1.482-483).

3.1.6 ἐλαία < *elaiwa 'olive-tree' could easily derive from an earlier *laiw- or *leiw- (*aleiw- > *elaiw-), and could then in turn be connected with ἀλείφω 'anoint' (cf. ἀμείβω beside ἀμοιϝα Schwyzer 1923:123.13) with *ἀλειϝω replaced by ἀλείφω because of the aorist ἄλειψα and the future ἀλείψω (< *aleiwsa/ō?). But clearly a Mediterranean origin for ἐλαία is still the best explanation (Frisk 1.480).

3.1.7 ἐλέγχω (*Il.* 9.522) 'disgrace, put to shame', ἔλεγχος (*Il.* 11.314) 'reproach, disgrace' is unexplained, but most etymologies start with the assumption that the /e/ is prothetic (Frisk 1.486-487). If so, prothesis must again be assumed before *lVnC- as in the case of ἐναλίγκιος. This case must be considered uncertain.[37]

3.1.8 Ἐλευσίς, the city northwest of Athens, and Ἐλευθεραί, a town north of Athens on the road to Thebes, are probably pre-Greek names (Frisk 1.492), but could have been originally *Leusis (or *Leuthis) and *Leutherai < IE *leudh- 'people' (Pok. 684-685). But if these names are pre-Greek, the prothesis developed (at least in these cases) on Greek soil.

[37] Seiler (1950:83,44) following Osthoff (*Morphologische Untersuchungen* 6[1910]8) has suggested connection of ἐλέγχω with ἐλαχύς.

3.1.9 ἐλεύσομαι (*Il.* 6.365) 'come' (fut.), ἐλευσίω· οἴσω (Hsch.). Prothesis seems reasonably certain in this word, for the best extra-Grk. cognates show initial /l/- (Frisk 1.492-493).

3.1.10 ἐλινύω (poetic and Ionic verb) 'keep holiday, take rest, repose' (sometimes written ἐλιννύω), ὀλινύει· λήγει, ἀργεῖ (Hsch.), though generally derived from forms with initial /l/ (Frisk 1.495), is too uncertain to support the assumption of prothesis. But if prothesis is present, then the verb must come from *linyuo, *linsuo, *lisnuo, no one of which is a particularly credible base form, unless it is a remodeled -nu- verb, hence from *leinumi.

3.1.11 ὀλιβρόν· ὀλισθηρόν, λεῖον, ἐπισφαλές (Hsch.: Frisk 2.376) and ὀλισθάνω (ὄλισθε *Il.* 23.774) 'I slip' (Frisk 2.377) constitute an exception to my rule since these words are indubitably to be connected with IE words with initial */sl/-. One would not, therefore, expect prothesis. Furthermore, ὀλισθάνω is unusual in that it provides us with the first instance of -/s/- taking the place of -*R*- in -*RC*-. But since the -/s/- clearly derives from -*dh*- (cf. Eng. *slide*), and since the -θάνω is clearly secondary, we can get over this second difficulty if we can assume that prothesis developed before proto-Grk. *libros and *lidh-, or better, *leibros (for we do not know the quantity of the -*i*- in this word) and *leidh-. These forms would develop, or could develop, according to the rule, to *əlibros and *əleidh-. Since *o*-color seems usual for the prothetic vowel before -*i*- vowels and diphthongs, *əl(e)i- > *ol(e)i-. But that still leaves the problem of the initial */sl/-. It is of course possible to assume *s*-movable in this root, as indeed Pokorny (Pok. 960-961) does, and that Grk. simply inherited an *s*-less form. This possibility is strengthened by the fact that *s*- in this family of words occurs certainly only in Germanic, Balto-Slavic, and Celtic forms, and hence may be a localized development not shared by Grk. And further, if *slei-dh- is form II of the root (cf. Benveniste 1935:192), form I (*seli-) does not occur, a fact which also encourages one to assume prefixal origin of the *s*- and an original root *lei- suffixed both by -*dh*- and -*b*-. While allowing the possibility that *lei- may lie behind ὀλισθάνω, it is nonetheless best to continue to work with *slei-. If we do, the only way to get around the problem of prothesis in a word once beginning with *sl- is to assume, at least for the moment, that prothesis in Grk. developed after the passage of /s/ > /h/ and its dissimilation by Grassmann's Law: *sleidh- > *hleidh- > *leidh- > *əleidh- > *oleidh-. We shall return to this matter below (6.1.2).

3.2.1 ᾿Αμάλθεια, the mythical goat, could show prothesis to a noun *malthos, but alpha privative is on the whole more likely (Frisk 1.84-85).

3.2.2 ἁμαρτάνω (Il. 10.372) 'miss the mark' could be included if the initial aspiration could be considered secondary, as it doubtless is (cf. νημερτής). We could then start from a root *mart- or *mert- > *mart- in *marteîn which in turn picked up a prothetic vowel, and because of structural similarity to λαχεῖν, etc., acquired also a present ἀμαρτάνω > ἁμαρτάνω (after ἅμα ?). But the word's history is too uncertain to allow of any such speculation. Prothesis cannot be excluded, but is unlikely (Frisk 1.87).

3.2.3 ἀμαυρός (Od. 4.824) 'dark, dim', ἀμαυρόω (Pi. P. 12.13, v.l. Hes. E. 693) has beside it the rare μαυρός or μαῦρος (Hdn. Gr. 1.193, Hsch., Gal. 18(2).518) and the verb μαυρόω (Hes. E. 325). The relation between these forms is obscure, but Frisk (1.88) assumes that ἀμαυρός is original, and that the shorter forms arose by an unexplained "Wegfall des Anlautvokals". He seems correct in this, but the word is for the rest effectively without etymology (Chantraine 1968:72), and to assume prothesis is unnecessary. The negative prefix seems most probable.

3.2.4 ἀμείνων (Il. 1.116) 'better' is also unfortunately without extra-Grk. cognates, but requires an earlier *(a)meinyōn (Frisk 1.91, Chantraine 1968:74), and as a result the /a/- can be of prothetic origin. Alpha privative seems most unlikely in this case, but no better explanation has been provided.

3.2.5 ἀμείρω (Pi. P. 6.26) 'bereave' ἀπαμείρω (v.l. Od. 17.322, Hes. Th. 801) is probably a secondary present to the aorists ἀμέρσαι ἀμερθῆναι from ἀμέρδω (Frisk 1.91).

3.2.6 ἀμέλδειν· τήκειν, στερίσκειν (Hsch.) derives from PIE *meld-, while μέλδομαι derives from *smeld- (5.1.2 below).

3.2.7 ἀμέργω (Sappho PLF 122) 'pluck, pull' with ἀμόργη 'watery part which runs out when olives are pressed', if connected with ὀμόργνυμι (above 2.2.6), and hence with Skt. mārjmi 'wipe off' (Frisk 1.92), is a sure case of prothesis. An o-grade form, μοργός, without prothesis is also attested from the Atticistic lexicographer Pausanias (H. Erbse, Untersuchungen zu den Attizistischen Lexika 160 = ADAW 1949:2[1950]), who cites a phrase from Kratinos: ἀμοργοί· πόλεως ὄλεθροι (fr. 214K, 210 Edmonds).

3.2.8 ἀμέρδω (Il. 22.58) 'deprive, bereave' has beside it the shorter, non-prothetic forms μέρδει· κωλύει, βλάπτει; μερθεῖσα· στερηθεῖσα (Hsch.). There are no sure cognates, but Frisk (1.92) mentions the possibility that Skt. mṛdnáti, mardati 'grind, crush' are related. If so, the /a/- is prothetic. We shall return below (6.3.3) to the question of the forms without prothesis.

3.2.9 ἀμεύομαι 'surpass, outstrip' occurs only in the future ἀ-μεύσεσθε (P. Fr. 23S) and the aorist ἀμεύσασθ' (Pi. P. 1.45), and is considered by LSJ to be the Doric equivalent of ἀμείβομαι. There are again no certain relatives in other languages, but if Lat. moveo, Lith. máuju 'strip off, tear off', Skt. mīvati 'push, shove', Hitt. mauszi 'fall' are related (Frisk 1.92), then the /a/- is prothetic.

3.3.1 ἀνάγκη (Il. 5.633) 'force, constraint, necessity' together with its derivatives, has no certain etymology (Frisk 1.101), but all attempts at etymological reconstruction suppose that the initial vowel is either original or developed from [n̥]. Prothesis is not to be assumed.

3.3.2 ἄνευ (Il. 13.556) 'without, away from', ἄνευθε(ν) (Il. 2.27) 'id.' could be considered a case of prothesis simply by extending the symbol consonant to include pause as well. This is not the usual explanation (comparison with Goth. inu < *enu 'without' and OHG ānu < *ēnu 'without', Skt. ánu 'along'— Frisk 1.106), but certainly seems possible. We should then postulate a proto-Grk. *neu consisting of the IE sentence negative *ne plus the particle *u(d) seen in Cypriote Greek ὔχηρος (=τὰ ἐπίχειρα: Schwyzer 1923.679.5) where it replaces ἐπί, and which has sometimes been supposed to occur in a number of Mycenaean forms (Chadwick 1963:251). Or *neu could contain the /u/ of οὗτος which is the same as the intensive particle u of Skt. só < sá u (PIE *só u — Frisk 2.450). This kind of derivation seems not impossible, and if correct, requires the assumption of prothesis. Perhaps, though, it is best to stick with the traditional etymology, and to assume that PIE *eneu > *aneu under the pressure of the negative prefix.

3.3.3 ἐνεγκεῖν, the Attic aorist of φέρω οἴσω, in order to be included would again necessitate considering /n/ a member of R and postulating a proto-Grk. root-form *nenk-. This latter is not usually assumed (Frisk 1.512-513), and parallelism with ἀλαλκεῖν leads rather to the assumption of *en-enk-, a form whose relatives are then discovered in Skt. perf. ān-ámśa 'I have reached' and OIr. t-ān-ac 'I came'. But this supposition of course destroys the immediate and natural assumption of relatedness with OCS nesǫ 'I carry', a connection one hates to give up. Rather we should assume that *nenkon is the reduplicating aorist of this root *nek- 'carry' which in Grk. developed a prothetic vowel.

3.3.4 ἐνιπή (Il. 3.438) 'rebuke, reproof' ἐνίπτω (Il. 3.438) 'reprove, upbraid' ἐνίσσω (Il. 15.198) 'attack, reproach' is of uncertain extra-Grk. connections, but the seemingly best analysis holds that these words are compounded with ἐν (Frisk 1.519). But an original *nīkʷ- (or *neikʷ-) is not impossible because the -i- is long (= /iy/). If we should decide in favor of *n(e)ikʷ-, ultimate connection with ὄνειδος 'reproach, rebuke' (above 2.3.1) becomes likely.

3.3.5 ἐνεῖκαι (Il. 5.885), the Ionic form of the aorist of φέρω οἴσω, is usually analyzed as ἐν-εῖκαι and connected then with ἵκω (Frisk 1.513). This seems the best explanation unless we favor some sort of dissimilation from *nenk-. *Neik-, though, and hence connection with Skt. ni 'lead', cannot be excluded a priori.

3.3.6 ὄνειρος (Il. 2.80) 'dream' seems an ideal candidate for inclusion among cases of prothesis and the postulating of a proto-Grk. *neiros: even the color of the prothetic vowel is right. But the existence of the old r/n stem ὄναρ (Il. 1.63), unless we wish to regard this word as secondary and artfully created, effectively destroys this possibility (cf. Frisk 2.393).

3.4.0 Before */w/-, because of the pan-Greek loss of /w/-, things are much more difficult. But the following cases at least are candidates for prothesis in terms of the rule given in 1.1.3.

3.4.1 ἄεθλος (Il. 3.126) 'contest' ἄεθλον (Il. 11.700) ἄθλιος (Thgn. 257) 'winning the prize' and more commonly, 'struggling, unhappy', perhaps a pessimistic interpretation of 'contending for a prize', hence 'losing', has no etymology (Frisk 1.22). But it does have the appearance of a word with prothetic vowel, and if we take 'prize' rather than 'contest' to be the original meaning, we may yet find a cognate for it in PIE *wedh- 'lead, take' (Pok. 1115-1116). For the semantics we may compare the meaning of 'win' of φέρομαι, and particularly phrases like ἄεθλον φέρομαι (Il. 9.127, 23.413) which show a connection between 'prize' and 'take (home) for oneself', and which indicate that ἄεθλον is the more original form and ἄεθλος a secondary interpretation of it. Formally, then, ἄεθλον is like a non-existent *φέρ-τ-λον > *φέρ-τ-ρον, a formation (and connection) rather surprisingly supported by Hesychius' gloss: φέρτρυς· ἄθλος.

3.4.2 ἀείδω (Il. 1.1) 'sing' ἀοιδή (Il. 2.595) 'song' ἀοιδός (Il. 18.604) 'singer' is somehow related to and connected with αὐδή according to Frisk (1.22-23), but in precisely what way is not clear. Perhaps the best solution, though there are major difficulties signaled by Frisk, is to assume (with Wackernagel 1953:654-655 = KZ 29.151-152) an original aorist *wewdeen which by dissimilation became *weideen, just as *wewpeen passed to *weipeen (Frisk 1.464); prothesis developed at some point, and *əweideen became generalized as a present stem. αὐδή derives from *υδή with the development of the purely Grk. initial vowel seen also in εὐρύς 'wide' beside Skt. urúḥ, and εὔκηλος 'free from care' beside ἔκηλος 'at rest'.[38] In this way connection can be made with the fairly widespread IE root *wed- (or *awed- according to Pok. 76-77) seen· in Skt. vad 'speak, say'. But perhaps connection with *wed- only appears to exist, and another etymology can be proposed which will not require the same elaborate derivation. First of all we must look at the meaning of the word ἀείδω in hopes of determining what its original meaning was: that it meant 'sing' from Homeric times on there can be no doubt, but it seems not to have had this as its principal meaning originally. Just as κλέος designates the content of the thing heard, and κλύω means 'to learn' (trans.) or 'be known' (intrans.) rather than physically 'to hear' (= ἀκούω), so ἀείδω seems to mean not so much 'sing' or 'make a noise' (= αὐδάω or φωνέω) as to 'tell, make known, convey information'. And of course the voice was the only readily available means of making things known. The constructions into which ἀείδω, a transitive verb, enters point in the same direction. μῆνιν ἄειδε θεά (Il. 1.1) means not: 'sing, goddess, the wrath', that is to say 'sing (rather than tell) a song', (when one thinks of it, a rather peculiar conceit), but rather: 'make known, tell of' (like ἔννεπε in Od. 1.1); and (Il. 9.189) ἄειδε δ᾽ ἄρα κλέα ἀνδρῶν (originally) meant 'was making known the reputations of men' (to Patroclus). Given this semantic matrix it seems indicated to seek a word meaning 'know' of the phonological shape *weid-. It is now clear that I feel that ἀείδω derives from an earlier transitive (causative) verb *weid- meaning 'make known', and therefore cognate with the Skt. root vid and the PIE root *weid-/*woid- 'know' but with the causative meaning of Skt. vedáyati 'make known'. For the formal relation *weidō 'cause to seem or be seen' *weidomai 'to be seen, appear, seem' *woida 'know', one of course will compare πείθω 'cause to believe' πείθομαι 'believe' πέποιθα 'believe, trust'.[39]

---

[38] On this development of a vowel before initial /u/ cf. Solmsen 1901:168-185 and Wackernagel's rule (1955:654) according to which all initial /u/- in PGrk. develop to */au/-. More on this below in 6.4.

[39] A striking semantic parallel is seen in the etymological connection of ἔννεπε with Eng. see (Pok. 897-898). ἔννεπε means 'cause to see, cause to know' → 'tell'.

3.4.3 ἀείρω (*Il.* 10.465) ἀέρρω (Sappho — *PLF* 111.3) αἴρω (Attic), fut. ἀρῶ (< *ἀερῶ), aor. ἤειρα ἀέρθην perf. ἄωρτο (*Il.* 3.272, 19.253) is rendered doubly difficult because the one word may be a blend of two earlier words (Frisk 1.23-24), and further because neither one has a reliable etymology: 1. ἀείρω means 'lift, raise' while 2. ἀείρω (only with συν and παρα) means 'tie together, join'. At least we can with Chantraine (1968:23) rejoin these two words, since there is nothing in the way semantically of doing so, and assume a base form *awer-. But this does not help much, and perhaps the best solution is simply to suppose some sort of connection with PIE *wer- 'binden, anreihen, aufhängen' (Pok. 1150-1152) and leave it at that: the /a/- could then be prothetic or possibly copulative. If prothetic, it must have developed in the aorist (*wersa) or the aorist passive (*werthēn), for a *weryo would not produce prothesis (below 5.9.0).

3.4.4 ἀέλλη (*Il.* 2.293) 'stormy wind' seems to derive from an earlier *awelya (cf. ἀείλη· πνοή [Hsch.]), and as such is a derivative in -/l/- of ἄημι 'blows'. It seems further connected with a Welsh word *awel* 'wind', and thus to contain original IE *awe-, and not *we-, with prothesis (Frisk 1.24-25). The same can be said also of ἀετμόν· τὸ πνεῦμα, ἄετμα· φλόξ (Hsch.) and ἀτμός (A. *Eu.* 138) 'steam, vapor', though ἀτμός (A. *Fr.* 206) seems to cause difficulty with this last form. All these words derive from PIE *awe-, not from *we-, and hence have original PIE */a/-, if we accept the connection with the Welsh word; or they have ἀ- either by analogy of the verb ἄημι (below 4.4.3), or are derived directly from ἄημι: prothesis as usually understood is not to be assumed in these forms, though we shall see that it is to be assumed in ἄημι.

3.4.5 ἄεμμα (Call. *Dian.* 10, *Ap.* 33) 'bow-string or bow' is, as Frisk says (1.25), a "künstliche Zerdehnung aus ἄμμα" 'knot, cord'.

3.4.6 ἀέξω (rare and poetic after the *Iliad*) 'increase, foster' has only present and unaugmented imperfect forms and few derivatives, while its close relative αὔξω (and αὐξάνω) 'increase', though not in Homer, is frequent throughout Grk. and has many derivatives. Extra-Greek etymological connections are many (Frisk 1.187-188, Chantraine 1968:141), though there is no direct equivalent of ἀέξω unless one wishes to believe that Skt. *vakṣáyati* 'let grow' derives from **aweks-* with loss of initial /a/ (cf. Wyatt 1970:27). But it is probably from another IE root **weg-* (Pok. 1117-1118) seen also in Lat. *vegeo* 'move, excite' and Goth. *wahsjan*, and hence not directly relevant. ἀέξω is either a purely Grk. formation to earlier αὔξω, or derives from PIE **weg-* and has undergone the influence of αὔξω. Prothesis is not involved any more than it was in ἀλέξω (3.1.2).

3.4.7 ἄεπτος (ἄαπτος *Il.* 1.567) is too uncertain in every way to be considered for inclusion among cases of prothesis. Its meaning ('invincible, resistless'), if really certain, would argue for an original negative compound (cf. Frisk 1.25).

3.4.8 ἄρδω (Hdt. 2.13) 'water', used in Attic in the present and imperfect only, contains a long initial vowel (Hdn. *Gr.* 2.109). And though Frisk (1.135) holds that the word's etymology is unknown, it seems perfectly acceptable to postulate an earlier **werdō* > **əwerdō* and seek an IE cognate of this form. There are a number of such, including Skt. *varṣati* 'it rains' and also Skt. *vāri* 'water'. Semantically the best connection is with Skt. *unátti*, 3rd plur. *undáti* 'wet, moisten' and formally with Lith. *vérdu vìrti* 'gush, simmer, cook' (Pok. 78-81). It seems further that **wer/wen*, extended by -/d/-, occurs both in ἄρδω and Lat. *unda* 'wave', a fact which suggests in turn that 'water' was originally **werd-/*wend-* ∿ **urd-/*und-*; as such it was formed very much like the word for 'heart': **ker-d-*. But **urd-* or **urōd-* generally experienced metathesis, thus yielding the normal IE root-form **uVdr-* ∿ **udVr-*. The assumption of prothesis in the Grk. word seems justified.

3.4.9 ἀίσθω occurs only twice (*Il.* 16.468, 20.403), and has thus far found no certain interpretation, though LSJ, in comparing ἄημι, translate 'breathe out', a meaning assumed also in the phrase: ἐπεὶ φίλον ἄιον ἦτορ (*Il.* 15.252). We cannot assume prothesis until a secure semantic interpretation and a reliable etymology are found.

3.4.10 ὀϊστός (*Il.* 4.125) 'arrow', Attic οἰστός, has no good etymology (Frisk 2.369), but again has the appearance of a prothetic form, and, if we take our cue from οἴγνυμι, may conceal an earlier *oweistos* < *weistos* (or possibly only *wistos*). We should then have to posit a verbal root *weis-* or *weidh-*, *weid-*, *weit-*, and assume that ὀϊστός is the -*to*- participle of that root. The original meaning of the word then would have been 'that which is — ', and would presumably have been used adjectively to modify ἰός 'arrow'. It is possible, no more, that ὀϊστός is connected with ἴεμαι 'hasten, be eager', and further with Skt. *véti* 'pursue, drive', Lith. *vejù výti* 'hunt, pursue', and possibly also with Hitt. *ui̯a-* (*u̯i̯a-*) '(her)-schicken' (Frisk 1.711).

3.4.11 Two further cases may belong here, though only difficulties in Homer suggest that they be included: Ὀϊλεύς Ὀϊλιάδης and Οἴτυλος (Chantraine 1948:116-117). There are a number of instances in our texts of uncertainty concerning Ὀϊλεύς: Zenodotus in *Il.* 12.365 and 13.203 read Ἰλιάδη-, and in 15.333 ὁ Ἰλῆος, 15.336 ὁ Ἰλεύς, thus suggesting that he knew of a tradition in which the man's name lacked an initial ὀ-. And if we should assume with Chantraine that the name derives from *ϝιλεύς, then we can account for the textual uncertainty by positing on the one hand a form with prothesis, Ὀϊλεύς > Οἰλεύς, on the other a form without, Ἰλεύς, both perhaps having something to do with the place-name Ἴλιος.

The other example is perhaps more certain. If we connect the Οἴτυλον of *Il.* 2.585 with the place-name Βείτυλον of *IG* V 1.935, we can explain the discrepancy in the diphthong (and the absence of digamma in Οἴτυλον) on the assumption that Βείτυλον (= ϝείτυλον without prothesis) is the correct local name for the place, and that original *weitulon* > *oweitulon* > Οἴτυλον in an area or dialect where prothesis was the rule. Both cases, if they are to be included, show *wei-* > *əwei-* > *owei-*, again with the /o/- expected before *Rei-* (2.4.13).

3.5 Of the above I feel that the following (broken down into a) most probable and b) probable), are relatively likely to contain a prothetic vowel: a) ἐλεύσομαι (3.1.9), ὀλιβρόν ὀλισθάνω (3.1.11), ἀμέργω (3.2.7), ἄεθλος (3.4.1), ἀείδω (3.4.2), ἄρδω (3.4.8); b) Ἐλευσίς (3.1.8), ἀμέρδω (3.2.8), ἀμεύσασθαι (3.2.9), ἄνευ (3.3.2), ἐνεγκεῖν (3.3.3), ἐνιπή (3.3.4). But of course the importance of this section consists not so much in identifying new cases of prothesis as it does in seeing whether the rules for prothesis need revision in the light of these examples. The answer is that three changes, all minor, must be admitted. 1) We must specify a stage of the Grk. language at which prothesis developed, for it is clear that it did not develop at all periods of the Grk. language. It seems at present that */sl/- must have already passed to */hl/- and have been dissimilated to /l/- by a following aspirate if we are to include ὀλισθάνω; more on this below. 2) If we include ἄνευ, we must include pause in the class C. 3) Finally, if we accept ἐνεγκεῖν, we no longer need to exclude nasals from the class R as we have been tempted to. This particular provision will receive its test below in 5.

APPARENT EXCEPTIONS
TO THE RULE FOR PROTHESIS

4.0 I have stated above the rule which accounts for, or which should account for, all cases of prothesis before resonants. There are, though, a number of words for which prothesis has been assumed, or could have been assumed, in the past which do not conform to the rule. We cannot leave this residue unmentioned and still claim that the rule given in 1.1.3 in fact accounts for all cases of prothesis and states all the environments in which prothesis occurs.

4.1.1 ἀλαπάζω (*Il.* 2.367) 'empty, drain; sack, destroy' ἀλαπαδνός (*Il.* 2.675) 'weak, feeble' beside λαπάσσω 'empty' in medical writers might be considered a case of prothesis (Frisk 1.64, Chantraine 1968:54). But extra-Grk. connections for this word do not exist, and the more or less inherently negative meaning of the word encourages one to think rather of the negative prefix than the prothetic vowel.

4.1.2 ἄλαστος (*Il.* 22.261) 'insufferable'. This example might have been included in section three, but was not because my rule makes no provision for prothesis before syllables closed by sibilant plus stop. The etymology of the word is unknown, as indeed is the real meaning, for its apparent meaning is a secondary inference from the nouns it modifies (πένθος, ἄχος; cf. ὁμοῖος 'equal for all' → 'evil' because of the nouns it modifies — Wyatt 1969b: 174-175), but the best assumption still seems the most obvious one: negative prefix plus λαστός to λανθάνω 'wer oder was nicht vergessen wird oder werden kann' (Frisk 1.64-65).

4.1.3 ἀλώπηξ (Archil. 86.2) 'fox'. Because of Lith. *lāpè*, Lett. *lapsa* 'fox' and Skt. *lopāśá-* 'jackal' one might be tempted to assume prothetic origin of the ἀ-. But these words are not directly comparable, so ἀλώπηξ has to be considered effectively without etymology (Frisk 1.83), unless (with Chantraine 1968:68) we assume the effects of taboo. My own guess would be to assume connection with Lat. *vulpēs* 'fox' as follows: *ulōpēks > *aulōpēks > ἀλώπηξ by dissimilation of lip-rounding caused by the following /o:/.[40]

4.1.4 ἐλελίζω (*Il.* 1.530) apparently had the original meaning 'turn or return (upon one's self)', hence 'coil, vibrate', and hence, too, it does not seem necessary to assume two distinct words (as Frisk does 1.488-489): 1. 'erschüttern' 2. 'herumdrehen'. For ἐλελίζω 'erschüttern' Frisk compares Skt. *réjate* 'tremble, quiver', *réjati* 'cause to tremble', Goth. *laikan* 'hop, spring', Lith *láigyti* 'wild herumlaufen'. He is almost certainly correct in his extra-Grk. connections, even though he has to make two somewhat questionable assumptions: 1) -ίξαι, -ίζω is not suffixal, but is part of the root; 2) we must start from a reduplicating aorist ἐ-λέ-λιξ-α, and assume that to this were formed the aorist passive ἐ-λελίχ-θην and the present ἐ-λελίζω: the initial ἐ- is then either prothetic or the augment mistakenly transferred to the present. Clearly, pro-thetic origin of the ἐ- is out according to my rules, and I feel that mistaken transferrals of the augment, though not to be discarded a priori, are extremely unlikely. What is needed is an explanation that will avoid these drawbacks while at the same time preserving the (probably correct) etymology. I suspect that all the attested forms of this word derive in fact from the past perfect ἐλέλικτο (*Il.* 11.39, 13.558) interpreted as an unaugmented reduplicating aorist or imperfect (cf. δέκτο to δέχομαι), possibly having some-thing to do with ἐλίσσω. We then follow Frisk's explanation. But if we adopt my initial step in the development, then we must posit a root *leig- to which would have been formed the following tense forms (if a present, etc., were ever actually created): *leigo (or *leigyo), *leiksa, *leliga or *leloiga, perf. mid. *leligmai. These forms would in the course of time have become: *əleigo,

<hr />

[40] For a parallel to this dissimilation of lip-rounding, cf. the various forms of the word 'furrow' (Frisk 1.77): αὖλαξ (ὦλαξ) but ἄλοξ < *ul-.

*əleiksa, *əle:liga or *əle:loiga, *əleligmai (cf. κατερήριπεν 'fall down' *Il.* 14.55 beside ἐρέριπτο *Il.* 14.15, and Kuryłowicz 1956: 269-272 for the origin of Attic reduplication in roots elsewhere showing the prothetic vowel). If this explanation is adopted, we can both keep the good etymology, and find further support in ἐλελίζω for my rule which predicts prothesis.

4.2.1 ἀμαρύσσω (Hes. *Th.* 827) 'sparkle, twinkle, glance', ἀμάρυγμα (Hes. *Fr.* 21.3, 94.6), ἀμάρυχμα (Sappho *PLF* 16.18) ἀμαρύττα· τοὺς ὀφθαλμούς Hsch. (ἀμάρυγγας — Latte), ἀμαρυγή (*h. Merc.* 45) 'sparkling, twinkling, glancing'. This word is usually connected with μαρμαίρω 'flash, sparkle, gleam', a connection which then requires that the ἀ- be prothetic. But this connection, which leaves much unexplained, cannot be considered certain, and the word remains effectively without etymology (Frisk 1.87). I have no suggestions.

4.2.2 ἀμάω (*Il.* 18.551) 'reap grain' in Homer always has a long vowel in the uncompounded forms, a short vowel in the compounded forms; Attic always has a short vowel, if, that is, ἀμάω (B) 'draw, gather' is considered a separate verb as it is by LSJ, Frisk (1.88-89) and Chantraine (1968:70). ἀμάω (A), translated by Frisk as 'schneiden', is usually connected with OHG *mäen* OE *mäwan* 'mow' on the assumption that these words also originally meant 'schneiden'. This assumption then of course requires that the ἀ- be prothetic. But it seems in the first place inadvisable to separate ἀμάω (A) from ἀμάω (B), even though this can be done. Rather the two words should be kept together and assigned the original meaning 'gather', though they had diverged sufficiently by Homer's day that ἀμάω (A), together with its compounds and derivatives had come to mean 'cut'. If the meaning 'gather' is assumed, then it would be most natural to assume that ἀ- comes from *sm̥, the copulative prefix. Whether the whole word derives from ἅμα 'at the same time, together with', the etymology Frisk prefers for ἀμάω (B), or whether it is a compound of ἀ- with some other word (possibly the Germanic cognates mentioned by Frisk for ἀμάω (A), I do not know. But the ἀ- is not prothetic in the sense of having arisen by anticipation of voice in the μ-.

4.2.3 ἀμύσσω (*Il.* 1.243) 'scratch, tear', ἀμυχή (Hp. *Epid.* 7.32) 'scratch, skin-wound', ἀμύξ (Nic. *Th.* 131) 'scratching, tearing' has no certain etymology (Frisk 1.97-98), for comparison with Lat. *mucro* 'sharp point, sword' (< *muk-ros*) and Lith. *mùšti* 'beat', OE *gemyscan* 'afflict, trouble', the only reason for assuming prothesis, is altogether too uncertain.

4.2.4 ἐμέ, enclitic με 'me' (acc.) is cognate with Lat. *mē*, Skt. *mā*, Goth. *mik*. The initial ἐ- comes from the nominative ἐγώ (Frisk 1.504), a development shared by Arm. *im* 'mei'.

4.3.1 ὀνίνημι (*Il.* 24.45), aor. ὤνησα (*Il.* 1.503) 'profit, benefit, help', ὄνειαρ (*Il.* 22.433) 'that which brings profit', ὄνησις (*Od.* 21.402) 'use, profit', Myc. *o-na-to* (PY Ea 29) 'lease', *o-na-te-re* (En 74.2) 'holders of *o-na-to*' (Chadwick 1963:226) lacks any sort of etymology (Frisk 2.395-396). Clearly the present ὀνίνημι is secondary, and all speculation must begin with the root-form *onā-*. To what this root is related we cannot say, but given the fact that it is a technical term already in Myc. times for an institution which the Greeks probably did not know before their arrival in Greece, Mediterranean origin is altogether most likely. *onā-* may have meant 'usufruct' or some such thing, a technical agricultural term, and then acquired more general meanings, first in the middle, 'use, enjoy'.

4.3.2 ὄνομαι (*Od.* 17.378), aor. ὠνοσάμην (*Il.* 14.95) 'blame, find fault with', ὀνοστός (*Il.* 9.164) 'to be blamed or scorned', ὄνοσις (Eust. 733.61) 'blame' has no sure extra-Greek cognates (Frisk 2.397), and only a mistaken connection with Skt. *nindati* 'blame' favors the assumption of prothesis.

4.4.1 ἀέλιοι· οἱ ἀδελφὰς γυναῖκας ἐσχηκότες, αἴλιοι· σύγγαμβροι (Hsch.), εἰλίονες (Pollux 3.32): οἱ δὲ ἀδελφὰς γήμαντες ὁμόγαμβροι ἢ σύγγαμβροι ἢ μᾶλλον συγκηδεσταὶ καὶ παρὰ τοῖς ποιηταῖς εἰλίονες seems best taken (Frisk 1.24) as cognate with ON *svilar* 'brothers-in-law whose wives are sisters' < *swelo-*, *sweliyo-*. The ἀ-, then, is copulative.

4.4.2 ἄεσα (*Od.* 3.151), contracted ἄσαμεν (*Od.* 16.367), always with νύκτα(ς) 'spend the night' (LSJ); ἀέσκω (Hdn. *Gr.* 1.436, *EM*

20.11) 'sleep'; ἀέσκοντο· ἀνεπαύοντο, ἐκοιμῶντο (Hsch.), has been variously explained. The currently most fashionable etymology (Frisk 1.25) connects these words with Skt. *vásati* 'stay overnight', Goth. *wisan* 'be', Arm. *gom* 'I am', and further, though less confidently, with Hitt. *ḫuišzi* 'he lives'; and within Grk. itself with ἄστυ 'town' and ἑστία 'hearth'. Assuming the semantic interpretation of ἄεσα to be correct, we must then further assume that the form is an aorist *ἄεσσα to a present ἀϝέσω, and that this present in turn continues an IE *wesō: prothesis, then, will have developed before *wesō (or *wehō). My rules do not predict prothesis in this environment, and indeed the example of *wesar 'spring' (6.3.1 below) excludes it, and another explanation must be found. There exists in Grk. another verb of similar meaning, ἰαύω (*Il.* 14.213) 'sleep, pass the night', ἰαύεσκον (*Od.* 5.154), which has the appearance of being a reduplicated present (it occurs generally in the present and imperfect) of a root *au(s)- seen in αὐλή 'open court' < *au(s)la, αὖλις 'place for passing the night' (Frisk 1.706, who mentions the possibility of connection with ἄεσα) < *au(s)lis. And if we do establish a root au(s)-, we can then easily account for ἄεσα by deriving it from *awessa, an aorist to *awesō, a form which would stand in the same relation to (ἰ)αύω as does ἀλέξω to ἀλκή (3.1.2) and ἀέξω to αὔξω (3.4.6). It may well be doubted that ἰαύω is related to Skt. *vásati* etc., but it is not impossible on the assumption either that Grk. *us- > *aus- (or *uh- > *auh- 6.4 below) or that Skt. *awes- > *wes- (Wyatt 1970:27).

4.4.3 ἄημι (*Il.* 5.526) 'blow', ἀήτης (*Il.* 15.626) 'blast, gale' (and ἄετμα, etc.— above 3.4.4) are quite clearly identical with Skt. *vāti* 'blows', Goth. *waian*, OCS *vějǫ* 'blow' and related to forms in -/nt/- in other languages such as Lat. *ventus*, Goth. *winds*, Toch. A *want*, Hith. *ḫuu̯ant-*, all meaning 'wind', and all probably in origin participial forms to *wē- (Frisk 1.26-27). The Grk. initial ἀ- is definitely prothetic, and definitely fails to conform to my rule. But it is possible that the monosyllabic character of this word provides the explanation for prothesis, for a number of forms do in fact have a closed syllable: participial forms like ἀέντες (*Il.* 5.526) and ἀέντων (*Od.* 5.478, 19.440), and the third plural of the present ἄεισι (Hes. *Th.* 875) < *awenti. Since third person forms of this verb (participles and infinitives aside) must effectively have been the only forms in use, we may suppose that the P-Grk. paradigm of this verb was: *wēti, *wēton, *wenti > *əwenti. This "paradigm", influenced doubtless by the participle *wents > *əwents, was leveled in favor of the longer form to *əwēti, *əwēton, *əwenti. Hence the development of the prothetic vowel in this case is again perfectly regular and predictable, and again we see that /n/ is a member of R.[41]

4.4.4 ἀΐω (*Il.* 15.130) 'perceive by the ear, hear' has a short initial vowel in Homer, but a long in Attic, generally in the compound ἐπαΐω 'give ear to'. Frisk (1.48-49) compares Skt. āvíṣ 'offenbar', and hence derives ἄιον from *awison. But if Schulze (1966: 344-349 = *KZ* 29.251ff.) is right in recovering a present ἀείω from: the Hesychian glosses ἄει· ἀκούει, ἄετε· ἀκούσατε, Euripides' (*HF* 773) ἐπάειν, Hesiod (*E.* 213):

ὦ Πέρση, σὺ δ᾿ ἄειε δίκης, μηδ᾿ ὕβριν ὄφελλε
(ἄκουε codd., ἄιε *EM* 43.6ff) and *Od.* 1.352:
τὴν γὰρ ἀοιδὴν μᾶλλον ἐπικλείουσ᾿ ἄνθρωποι
ἥ τις ἀειόντεσσι
(ἀκουόντεσσι codd. ἀειδόντεσσι Pl. *Rep.* 4.424b)
then it may well be that the earliest Grk. form of this word was *weis- or some such. In the absence of an extra-Greek cognate for such a root, however, the connection favored by Frisk seems preferable, even though causing some difficulties.

4.4.5 οἴομαι 'forebode, presage; think, suppose' shows a bewildering number of forms which include the presents οἴομαι (*Il.* 5.644) οἶμαι (Att., trag.) ὀίομαι (*Od.* 10.193) ὀΐω (*Il.* 8.536) οἴω (*Il.* 5.252) ὀίω (*Il.* 1.558); the aorists ὀίσατο (*Od.* 1.323) ὀισθείς

---

[41] The ḫ- in the Hitt. word is still problematic and interesting, but must now be investigated for itself alone. The rules governing the development of /h/ before /w/ in Hitt. seem to differ from those of Grk., though ḫuiš- (ḫueš-) 'live' obeys the same rule as does ἑστία (< *westia) with aspiration developing before -/s/- plus voiceless consonant.

(*Il.* 9.453) οἰηθείς (Att. and Ion. — E. *IA* 986). Frisk (2.366) deduces from the -/s/- of the aorist passive that the original form of the root was **owis-*, and the present οἴομαι < **owisyomai*. This hypothetical construct, if one can assume the shortening of /i:/ in hiatus, will take care of all the forms, but fails to find any related forms in other IE languages. Szemerényi (1964:217-218), noting this difficulty, separates ἀίω from Skt. *āvíḥ* and compares οἴομαι with *āvíḥ*: οἴομαι < **ōwisyō* or **ōwisō* 'seems, thinks, becomes clear'. Either of these scholars may be right, but perhaps another possibility might be suggested. οἴομαι looks and in many respects behaves like οἴγνυμι, and the suspicion therefore arises that it in fact derives from an earlier **oweis-*, represented in Homeric manuscripts as οἴ-. This supposition will then allow a present **oweisō*, and will not demand the ad hoc and unnecessary assumption of **owisyō*, an assumption rendered a priori unlikely by the fact that to -*yo*- presents we expect aorists in -ην, not in -θην: μαίνομαι : ἐμάνην, but λέγω : ἐλέχθην. Hence the original paradigm of this word was probably **oweisō* **ow(e)isthēn*. And given such an original form we are again encouraged to think of a still earlier form **weis-* (or **weid-*), and to regard **oweisō* as yet another case of prothesis. Unfortunately again we can find no extra-Greek support for **weis-*.[42]

4.5 We therefore see that none of the instances of prothesis which have been supposed or suggested in the past and which fail to conform to my rule are to be given serious consideration. On the other hand we have found that two additional cases do conform to the rule: ἐλελίζω (4.1.4), ἄημι (4.4.3), this latter confirming that

---

[42] If one connects οἴομαι with Skt. *āvíḥ*, there is no need to assume that the /a:/ points to earlier PIE */o:/, for **owis* would pass to *āvíḥ* in Skt. by Brugmann's Law (as indeed would **awis-* cf. Wyatt 1970:74). More on the etymology of this word in n. 57 below. Szemerényi's assumption of syncope: οἴομαι > οἶμαι (1964:216-218) is unlikely to be correct, for syncope occurs only (or generally) in οἶμαι, a form generally used parenthetically. It seems therefore best to assume that it is a form abstracted from the equally parenthetical ἐγῷμαι where the contraction is regular (cf. ᾤμην). Put in the shape of a formula: ἐγῷμαι + οἴομαι → οἶμαι.

-/n/- is a member of R: and two further cases which might conform and hence contain prothesis: ἀΐω (4.4.4) and ὀΐω (4.4.5). The rule predicts all cases of prothesis.

CASES IN WHICH
PROTHESIS FAILS TO DEVELOP

5.0 It is now time to turn my rule around and regard it as essentially a prothesis-predicting device, making the stronger claim that not only does prothesis occur only under the conditions specified, but that it always occurs when these conditions are fulfilled. Clearly this means 1) including all cases of an initial vowel appearing in the relevant environment, a task we attempted in 3; and 2) investigating all cases where my prediction fails. First we shall look into those cases of $\text{Re}\begin{bmatrix} RC \\ CR \end{bmatrix}$ which pass to $\text{Re}\begin{bmatrix} RC \\ CR \end{bmatrix}$ counter to the rule which would predict *əRe-*. These are the most crucial cases, for as we have seen (2.5) this environment is most favorable to the development of prothesis. The corpus of relevant examples will be Frisk's *GEW*, and I shall in this section include all instances of *RVCC-* (where *V* represents non-rounded vowel), regardless of the constitution of *-CC-*, for, though only certain instances of *-CC-* are relevant to my rule as stated, I should like also to be able to specify in rule form where prothesis does not occur. It may be that the environments I have isolated for the occurrence of prothesis are not positive environments, but are rather the residue left over from the application of another rule. In order not to exclude this possibility I include all cases of non-rounded vowel plus *-CC-*.

5.1.1 First a number of types of words must be excluded. Clearly not to be included here are those words which have no secure etymology. We may presume that most of them are not IE, but were borrowed into Grk. after the PGrk. period, after, that is to say, the rule for prothesis had ceased to operate. References in parentheses are to Frisk's *GEW*: λευρός 'smooth' (2.109-110: unerklärt), λεύω 'stone' (2.110: probably to λᾶας 'stone'), μείλιχος 'gentle, kind' (2.194-195); μέλκιον· κρήνη, νύμφαι, παίγνιον (Hsch. 2.202), μέλπω 'celebrate with song and dance' (2.204: ohne Etymologie), μέρμις 'cord, string' (2.211), μεστός 'full' (2.215: unerklärt), μέσφα 'until' (2.215-216); νεῖκος 'quarrel' (2.297: ohne sichere Etymologie), νέκταρ 'nectar' (2.300-301: ohne sichere Etymologie); Εἴλωτες 'helots' (1.462), εἱμάδες· ποιμένων οἰκίαι (Hsch.: 1.462).

5.1.2 Another group of words which is not to be considered in matters concerning prothesis is that which at one time had IE initial *sR-.[43] Among cases of this type of word may be included: λεῖμαξ (2.97) λειμών 'meadow' (2.98-99); μειδιάω 'smile' (2.193-194), μείρομαι 'receive as one's due' (2.196-197), μέλδομαι 'soften by boiling' (2.199-200), cognate not with Eng. *melt* but with Eng. *smelt*; μέρμερος 'causing anxiety' (2.210-211); νείφει 'snows' (2.298-299), though this word might better have been included in 5.1.4 below among words whose proto-Grk. shape was other than that seen in Classical times: in PGk. the only shape of this root may have been *nigʷh- (cf. νίφα), and *neigʷh- not yet known; νευρά 'string, bowstring' (2.308-309); ἔθνος 'number of people living together, people' (1.448-449), ἕξ 'six' (1.527-528), ἕρμα 'prop, support' (1.561-563).

5.1.3 Words that are clearly non-IE are not to be included among exceptions to the rule predicting prothesis: λείριον 'lily' (2.100-101); μέλκα 'cooling food made from sour milk' (2.202), μέλλαξ 'youth, lad' (late — 2.202), μέσκος· κώδιον, δέρμα. Νίκανδρος (Hsch.: 2.213), μέσπιλον 'medlar' (2.215); ϝέλχανος, name of Zeus on Crete (1.503-504).

5.1.4 A number of words, though IE, did not occur in PGrk. in a shape relevant to the rule, the shape they had in classical times. /w/ will not appear in this category and the next because of various uncertainties resulting from its prehistoric loss. λείπω

---

[43] These examples might better have been postponed for further discussion and not introduced here because they presuppose an argument to be presented later. I am at present, however, interested only in isolating for more extended treatment cases inimical to my argument.

'leave' (2.99-100); though the root *lik^w- is very widespread in IE languages, present formations are various (Skt. ríṇákti, Lat. linquo beside Goth. leihan), while the aorists are the same: ἔλιπε, Skt. áricat, Arm. elikʿ, all from PIE *$elik^wet$). These facts show that the inherited form of the root was an aoristic *lik^w-, and that all present forms are secondary.[44] *$leik^w$- either did not exist, or was not the basic form of the paradigm, at the time prothesis developed. λείτωρ 'priest' (2.101) is attested only late, and may have derived from PGrk. */le:/-. λευγαλέος 'wretched' (2.108) is a secondary, probably poetic, derivative in -αλέος to λυγρός 'id.'. μείγνυμι 'mix' (2.192-193) is clearly a secondary present formed to the original form of the root seen in the aorist μιγῆναι and the adverb μίγα 'mixed or blended with'.

5.1.5 A similar category is composed of words in which prothesis is not present because of the analogy of other forms of the same root without prothesis. Here we may include: Att. μείζων, earlier and Ionic μέζων, 'larger' (2.189-190) after μέγας; νεκρός 'corpse' (2.299-300) beside νέκυς and νέκες· νεκροί (Hsch.). But the second case contains -/kr/-, and it may turn out that this cluster does not close a preceding syllable, and as a result does not favor the development of prothesis.

5.2.0 Nonetheless there remain a number of cases which seem to go against my rule, and which cannot be comfortably included in the categories established above.

5.2.1 λείβω 'pour', λεῖψαι should appear as *əleib- according to

---

[44] This supposition of course flies in the face of generally accepted theories of IE root structure which hold that normal grade (full grade) forms are original and reduced grade forms secondary to them. But this position is untenable, at least in the cases of /i/ and /u/ diphthongs, since the unaccented form of *$leik^w$- should be *$līk^w$-, with vowel contraction, and not *lik^w- with loss of a vowel. The opposite assumption, however, namely that */e/ and */o/ were inserted later, both accounts for IE */e/ ∼ Ø ablaut (which arose in a period when the IE accent contained a strong component of stress); and the pitch accent of late IE which arose when */e/ and */o/ were inserted in imperfective forms before */i/ and */u/, thus giving rise to a falling (circumflex) pitch. More on this in Wyatt 1970:56-59.

my rules, for the word seems definitely IE (Frisk 2.96-97), and definitely connected with OCS *lьjǫ*, Lith. *líeju* 'pour' and Lat. *lībāre* 'pour out'. But beside the *e*-grade forms there exist also *o*-grade forms (λοιβή 'drink offering' — *Il.* 9.500; λοιβᾶται· σπένδει, θύει [Hsch.]) and a number of zero-grade forms (*λίψ λιβός λίβα 'stream' A. *Eu.* 54, λίψ 'the Southwest wind' Hdt. 2.25, λιβάς 'spring, fount, stream' S. *Ph.* 1215). It is clear that the earliest Grk. form could have been either the full-grade or the zero-grade, and Frisk is uncertain which to assume. For my argument it really matters little, since an appeal to the analogy of the zero-grade forms would be sufficient to account for the lack of prothesis. But since Homer has the phrase ὄφρα λείψαντε (*Il.* 24.285 = *Od.* 15.149) with long (voiceless) /l/-, we may assume that *lib- > *hlib- was the original Grk. form, and that the present *hleibō was formed to this *hlib-.

λεῖος 'smooth' (*Il.* 4.484) seems cognate with Lat. *lēvis* 'smooth' and hence (Frisk 2.99) from an original *leiwos. But since Lat. *i*-stem adjectives are usually from old *u*-stems, we should imagine rather an original *lēyu- which develops in Lat. to *lēyuis > *lēüis > *lēwis, but in Grk. to *lēyuos > *leiwos > *leios. What the PGrk. form will have been we cannot tell, but *leywos seems most likely. Thus far we have not made any guess as to whether -*SS*- is a subclass of either -*CS*- or -*SC*-; but we cannot yet, and shall save discussion of this matter till later. For the moment, if Frisk is right in connecting λεῖος with λείμαξ, the original PGrk. form of λεῖος must have been *sleiwos < *slēyu- (or *slewyos).

λείχω (Hdt. 4.23), λείξω (Lxx *Mi.* 7.17) ἔλειξα (A. *Eu.* 106) 'lick up', λειχήν (A. *Ch.* 281) 'lichen' (frequently written λιχήν in mss.), λιχανός (Hp. *Art.* 37) 'licking' and other zero-grade derivatives (there are no *o*-grade forms in Grk.) is clearly an IE inheritance (cf. Lith. *liežiù*, OCS *ližǫ*, Lat. *lingo*, OIr. *ligim*, Skt. *léhmi lihmáḥ* < *léighmi *lighmés, all meaning 'lick' — Frisk 2.102). And clearly *leigh- in Grk. should result in *əleigh-. Hence λείχω remains a problematic exception, unless we can assume Grk. leveling of an earlier *əleik^hō : lik^héen (< *ligh-) > λείχω : λιχεῖν, a supposition rendered possible, but no more than that, by the clearly secondary nature of the Balto-Slavic (-*yo*) and Lat. (nasal infix) presents.

λευκός 'light, bright, clear' together with all its derivatives shows the *e*-grade in Grk., and the *e*-grade can be supposed also in Skt. *rocá*- 'shining' to *rócate* 'shine' (Frisk 2.108-109), though we should rather expect the *o*-grade in both λευκός and *rocá*-, a grade perhaps to be found in Lat. *lūcus* 'grove', Lith. *laũkas* 'field', OHG *loh* 'bewachsene Lichtung', Skt. *loká*- 'open space'. There are zero-grade forms (cognate with Skt. *ruc*- 'light'— Frisk 2.148-149) which we may consider basic to the entire family: λύχνος (*Od*. 19.34) 'lamp' (< *luksnos*), ἀμφιλύκη (Il. 8.433) 'half-light, morning twilight', and the late λυκαυγής (Heracl. *All.* 7) 'at the grey twilight', λυκόφως (Ael. *NA* 10.26) 'twilight' together possibly with λυκάβας (*Od*. 19.306) 'passage of time', Λυκηγενής (*Il*. 4.101) an epithet of Apollo. The development will have been *luk- > *hluk- → *hleuk-, either as I have put it, or by analogy: sc.

$$*\text{leuk-} > *\text{əleuk-}$$
$$\phantom{*\text{leuk-}} > \quad *\text{hleuk, *hluk-}$$
$$*\text{luk-} > *\text{hluk-}$$

Clearly λεύσσω < *leukyo 'look, gaze upon' is secondary to *luk- or *leuk-, and, because not found elsewhere, a purely Grk. formation (cf. Frisk 2.110). This case and the last therefore probably belong in 5.1.4 above.

λέχριος (S. *OC* 195) 'slanting, crosswise' has beside it λικριφίς (*Il*. 14.463, *Od*. 19.451) 'crosswise, slanting' looks like an IE word and acts like one (cf. its ablaut partner λοξός Hp. *Off.* 11 'slanting, crosswise'), but has no IE cognates (Frisk 2.112), and hence very likely belongs in 5.1.1 above.

5.2.2 μεῖραξ (Cratin. 301) 'young girl', μειράκιον (Antiphon 3.3.11) 'lad, stripling', possibly from a noun *μεῖρος, seems a certain cognate of Skt. *máryaḥ* 'young man', and hence originally from *mery-. This form of course brings us again to the question of whether -*RR*- is a member of -*RC*- or -*CR*-.

μείων (*Il*. 3.193) 'lesser, less', also in this form in Doric dialects (Schwyzer 1923:179 — Gortyn, 62.1.114 — Heraclea), if connected with Skt. *mināti* 'lessen, injure', *mīyate* 'decrease, pass away' (Frisk 2.197-198), must derive from **meiyon*; or if connected, as now generally supposed (Chadwick 1963:220), with Myc. *me-u-jo* (KN Ak 612), *me-wi-jo* (KN Ak 611) = [mewiyōn] or [meuyōn], from **meuyōn*. In either event the question of *-RR-* again arises, a question which the Homeric scansion: ἀλλὰ πολὺ μείων (*Il.* 2.529) may help to answer.

μέλλω (*Il.* 10.326) 'be destined or likely to' ἤμελλον (Hes. *Th.* 898) ἠμέλλησα (Thgn. 259) is thought to derive from earlier **melyō* (Schwyzer 1939:715), but this **melyō* has no certain explanation (Frisk 2.202-203), and hence probably belongs rather with the words in 5.1.1. If included here, though, the question of *-RR-* again comes up. The augment ἠ- seems secondary, and not the contraction product of augment plus prothetic vowel: sc. **e-əmellon* > ἤμελλον (cf. 5.5 below).

μέσος, epic μέσσος, Boeot. μέττος 'middle' clearly derives from **metsos* < **medhyos* (Frisk 2.214-215). **-dhy-* had already passed to **-ts-* in this word by proto-Grk. times, and as a result, μέσος does not provide an instance of aspirate plus **/y/* which should have occasioned prothesis (5.9.1 below). On the theoretical foundations underlying the assumption that **-dhy-* > **-ts-* is early, cf. Hamp 1960:187-190, Wyatt 1969, Nagy 1970 ch. 3, particulary 123-127.

μέτρον (*Il.* 12.422) 'measure, rule' is generally connected with Skt. *māti* 'measure' (< PIE *mēti*) and more immediately with Skt. *mātrā* 'measure' (Frisk 2.220-221), whose most direct cognate, though, is seen in Grk. μήτρα 'register of house-property at Tarsus and Soli' (POxy. 1802.58) and ἐρεσιμήτρην· τὴν γεωμετρίαν (Hsch.). Given this discrepancy in the vowel it is probably best to connect μέτρον with the IE root **med-* seen possibly in μέδιμνος and certainly in Germanic words for 'measure' like Goth. *mitan*, OE *metan* and in Grk. μέδομαι (Frisk 2.190-191). Frisk is quite right in stating that **medtron* would have given **mestron*, so I assume that **med-ron* (cf. δῶρον to δίδωμι) > **metron* by analogical assimilation to other words in *-tron*, and perhaps also under the direct influence of μήτρα. Whatever the case, this word, like νεκρός (5.1.5) contains *-TR-*, a cluster which in later times does not close a preceding syllable, and which, therefore, may not be includable in -CR-.

5.2.3 νεβρός (Il. 4.243) 'fawn' is connected by Frisk (2.296) with Arm. nerk, -oy 'color' and further with IE *(s)negʷro- on the assumption of an original meaning 'colored, motley'. This etymology is not convincing, but if correct, s-movable is in the picture.

νειός (Il. 10.353) νεός (X. Oec. 16.10) 'fallow-land' may derive from earlier *neiwos and be connected with OCS njiva 'field' (Frisk 2.297-298). Again the question of -RR- arises, but the etymology after all is uncertain.

Νέστωρ (Il. 1.247), the Homeric hero, has a name generally connected with the root *nes- 'return' (Frisk 2.304-306), but it is just as likely that the name has something to do with the Neda river in Messenia: *nedtor > *nestor. -/st/- has not yet found a place in -CC-.

νεύω (Il. 13.133) 'incline in any direction' is connected by Frisk (2.309) with Lat. -nuō < *-newō 'nod' and a base form *neusō or *neusyō set up for Grk., a base form which is supposed also to account for νυστάζω 'be half asleep, doze', νευστάζω 'nod' and νυστάζω 'prick, stab'. But in order to accommodate all these forms comfortably, we should have to assume as the basis for all the Grk. forms a root *nus-, a phonetic sequence which does not admit prothesis.

νεφρός (Ar. Ra 475) 'kidneys' is definitely connected with Festus' glosses nefrones nebrundines, and most likely also with OHG nioro MidE nēre, OSwed. niūre, and hence from PIE, or at least western IE, *negʷhro- (Frisk 2.310). If so, this word constitutes an exception to my prothesis rule.

5.3.0 With initial */w/- things are more difficult for the reasons mentioned above in 2.4.14, but I shall nonetheless list all those forms which might reasonably be expected to show prothesis, even though the reasons given in 2.4.14 will in most cases suffice to account for its absence.

5.3.1 ἔθρις (cod. ἐθρίς)· τομίας, κριός (Hsch.) beside ἴθρις· σπάδων, τομίας, εὐνοῦχος (Hsch.), ἄθρις (Suid.) ὄθρις (Zonar.). Frisk ac-

counts for the uncertainty of the initial vowel by appealing to its
nonliterary character, and assumes that /e/ was the original
vowel color, thus enabling him to compare the word with Skt.
vádhri- 'castrated, emasculated' (Frisk 1.449). His etymology is
doubtless correct, but ἄθρις (for *ἀ̂θρις?) almost certainly represents /a:tʰris/ < *awetʰris with prothetic vowel; ἔθρις, then, is
the restored original form with /a/- removed because taken to be
the falsely or unnecessarily placed negative prefix. About ἴθρις and
ὄθρις I do not know.

5.3.2 εἴκω (*Il.* freq.) 'give way, retire' shows no sign of prothesis
unless we should wish to include ἔειξα (Alcm. 31). The word's
etymology is, in the end, unknown, though Frisk (1.454) attempts
to connect forms pointing to *weig-* like Skt. *vijáte* 'flee before,
yield' and OE *wīcan* OHG *wīhhan* 'give way'.

5.3.3 εἶλαρ (*Il.* 7.338) 'covering, shelter, defence', if from
welwar, again gives -*RR*-, for which we might expect prothesis.
But the etymology is uncertain, and early dissimilation to *elwar*
possible (Frisk 1.455).

5.3.4 εἰλύω (*Il.* 5.186) 'enfold, enwrap' is clearly connected with
Skt. *vṛṇóti*, and hence encourages the idea that the Grk. form
derives from *welnuō* (Frisk 1.461-462). Again -*RR*- is involved,
and again prothesis might be expected. But in fact the constant
length of the -/u:/-, and the fact that Homer knows no present to
this verb (though he does have the future εἰλύσω *Il.* 21.319),
taken together indicate that all these forms derive from *wewlu-
mai* > *weilumai*, the perfect middle of the verb ἐλύω (*Il.*
23.393) 'wind, wrap around' < *weluo*. Traces of digamma in
this word are faint (Chantraine 1948:131, Schwyzer 1939:649), so
it is possible that the perfect in fact derives from *ewlūmai*, either
with dissimilation of the first /w/- or with the /e/- reduplication
used before */wl/-; we will provide still another possible explanation in note 55 below.

5.3.5 εἷμα (*Il.* 18.538) 'garment' (Frisk 1.521), ἕννυμι (*Il.* 5.905)
'put on clothes', ἐσθής (*Od.* 1.165) 'clothing', ἔσθος (*Il.* 24.94)
'garment' (Frisk 1.521-522) all derive from the widespread IE

root *wes-. The present ἕννυμι is clearly secondary to the aorist *wessa, and we now have evidence that /s/ is not a member of R in -RC- or of C in -CR-: if it were, we would expect prothesis. In fact, as we shall see later (6.3), /s/, by inducing initial aspiration, prevents prothesis.

5.3.6 The etymology of εἶρος (Od. 4.135) 'wool' is not certain, but if Lat. vervex 'wether' is related (Frisk 1.468-469), then we require a base form *werwos which may have yielded *erwos by dissimilation.

5.3.7 εἴρω (Od. 2.162) 'say', aor. (?) εἶρεν (B. 16.20), perf. εἴρημαι (Il. 4.363) stems from a root *wer- 'say' seen in Lat. verbum 'word', etc. (Frisk 1.470-471). Only the present is relevant to the rule (and the perfect, if not from *ewrēmai > εἴρημαι), and it is clearly a secondary creation, formed well after the period during which prothesis developed.

5.3.8 εἴσομαι (Il. 14.8) 'rush, hasten' is clearly the future of ἵεμαι (ἐ)είσατο (LSJ, Frisk 1.472), and as such must represent earlier *wi:somai, hence must contain the prothetic vowel: *wi:somai > *ewīsomai > *εἴσομαι, traces of which can still be seen (possibly) in the aorist ἐείσατο (Il. 4.138 — for εἴσατο), if, that is, we take this form to be the unaugmented aorist of the verb and not the augmented.

5.3.9 ἕλμινς (Hp. Morb. 4.54) and ἕλμις (Arist, HA 602ᵇ26) 'worm' either has no etymology, or is a deformation of PIE *kʷrmi- after the root *wel- seen in εἰλέω (Frisk 1.501).

5.3.10 ἔργον (Il. 1.294) 'work' and ἔρδω (Il. 4.37) 'do' < *werg- (Frisk 1.548-549) both should show prothesis but do not, while ἕσπερος (Il. 22.318) 'evening' < *wesp- (Frisk 1.575) and ἑστία (S. El. 881), Homeric ἱστίη (Od. 14.159) 'hearth' < *west- (Frisk 1.576-577) should not because of the aspiration-inducing -/s/-. We might also expect prothesis in εἶπον (Il. 1.68) 'I said' < *weup- (Frisk 1.464).

5.4.0 In many cases prothesis fails to develop before */w/-. We have seen some of the reasons for this above (2.4.14), but it is

possible that we can substantiate the notions of 2.4.14 by un-
covering further traces of the former presence of prothesis. It is
possible, for instance, to interpret apparently augmented aorists
and imperfects rather as forms with the prothetic vowel. The
following cases are possibilities: ἔειπε (*Il.* 2.194) 'said', ἐείσατο
(*Il.* 15.415) 'went' (5.3.8 above), ἐείσαο (*Il.* 9.645) 'seem' (to
εἴδομαι — 2.4.12 above), ἔεργεν (*Il.* 4.130) 'kept off' (to ἐέργω —
2.4.3 above), ἐέλδετο (*Od.* 4.162) 'wanted' (to ἐέλδομαι — 2.4.4
above), ἐέλπετο (*Od.* 23.345) 'wanted' (to ἐέλπομαι — 2.4.7
above), ἔερδον 'did' (Solon in *Ath. Pol.* 12.3, to ἔρδω — 5.3.10
above). Alcman's ἔειξε has already been mentioned (5.3.2). If we
allow these words as evidence of prothesis, then the seemingly
anomalous absence of prothesis in εἶπον is seen to result from the
(analogical) loss of prothesis rather than to its having failed to
develop.

5.5.0 The lengthened augment ἠ- has long been connected with
similar long augments in Skt. (Schwyzer 1939:653 following
Wackernagel 1953:583-587 = *KZ* 27:272-276), but it is unlikely
that this connection is correct. In the first place, whatever the
explanation of the Skt. phenomenon may be (it probably is a
vrddhi strengthening of the root in augmented tenses like that
seen before /i u r/ — *icchāti* but *áicchat* 'wish'), the augment *ā*-
appears before /v y r n/, while in Grk. it appears only before
/w/-. Furthermore it is rare and sporadic in Skt., restricted to the
Veda, and hence more than likely to be connected rather with
other Vedic irregular lengthenings than with Grk. augments. In
Grk. the augment ἠ-, though not constant before */w/- as
Wackernagel thought, is constant in those verbs in which it
appears. The Skt. development is to be treated for itself alone, and
the Grk. ἠ- is to be regarded as the contraction product of the
augment ἐ- and the prothetic vowel, a fact first ascertained (to my
knowledge) by G. Meyer (Meyer 1896:556).

5.5.1 Meyer's view has not found wide acceptance, but perhaps, if
we can show that the long augment occurs only in those
environments in which prothesis developed, and not in those
environments in which it did not develop, we may be able to

provide the needed confirmation. It is best to start with those cases in which prothesis is reasonably assured, and see whether the augment is indeed long. Clearly only words with initial */w/- are relevant here, for prothesis remained before the other resonants. ἔργω εἵργω (2.4.3 above) is an exception in that the aorist is εἷρξα (E. *Ba.* 443) and the impf. εἷργον (Th. 1.106). But this exception will later (6.3.3) turn out to confirm the rule because we shall see that prothesis develops before *wer- only when a voiced or aspirated consonant follows.

ἐέλδομαι (2.4.4 above) never appears augmented, while ἤλπετο (*Il.* 15.539, 701), usually emended to ἔλπετο, may well be the correct form < *eəwelpeto (to ἐέλπομαι — 2.4.7). In any event the aorist of ἐλπίζω is always ἤλπισα (Hdt. 8.24, S. *Ph.* 1175) < *eəwelpisa.

εἰλέω (2.4.8 above), a secondary form, has the expected aorist εἴλησα (Lxx 4Ki 2.8), but the primary form εἴλω has the aorist ἠλσάμην (Semon. 17) from *eəwels- (2.4.8 above).

εἴδομαι (2.4.12 above) has no aorist indicative forms (εἶδον < *ewidon without prothesis), but long augmented forms do occur in the pluperfect. ἤείδης ἤείδη (*Il.* 22.280, *Od.* 9.206) > ᾔδη (*Il.* 1.70) and Attic ᾔδη (S. *Ant.* 18) is the unreduplicated (but augmented) pluperfect to the equally unreduplicated οἶδα, and comes from earlier *eəweidea.

οἴγνυμι (2.4.13 above) clearly had a long augment, as is proved by the Attic forms with metathesis of quantity: ἀνέῳξα (Ar. *V.* 768, Th. 2.2). If we are to accept the evidence of Attic at face value, the word must have developed: *weig- > *oweig- > *ewoig- (with metathesis of the vowels) > *eewoig- > *ēwoig- > *eōig-, a strange and complicated development. But it is possible that ω forms without augment such as ὠΐγνυντο (*Il.* 2.809, 8.58), ὦιξε (*Il.* 6.298), ὦξε (*Il.* 24.457), ἀνῷξα (Hdt. 1. 68, Theoc. 14.15) are genuine, and reflect *weig- > *oweig- > *eoweig- > *ōweig- > *ō(e)ig- > *ōig-. In that event the Attic forms will not show metathesis of quantity, but will have a secondary augment added as in ἐώθουν (note 45 below).

Clearly ἀείδω (3.4.2), ἀείρω (3.4.3), ἄρδω (3.4.8) and οἴομαι (4.4.5) have long augments because prothesis remained in these words. We may imagine that the augment of ἄησι would have been long also had the verb ever appeared augmented. In addition to these certain cases there are also cases in which the augment ἠ- reflects the former presence of a prothetic vowel subsequently lost. The long augment is our only evidence for the former presence of prothesis.

ἠργαζόμην ἠργασάμην (Attic inscc. IVc. — LSJ) are the regular secondary tenses of ἐργάζομαι 'work, labor', (though later εἰ- forms also occur in mss.) and represent the contraction of *eəwerga-. Hence prothesis once appeared before *werg- as predicted. Why there is no trace of it in ἔργον I do not know.

ἥκειν (Ar. Av. 1298), the pluperfect to ἔοικα 'be like' beside the (early) remodeled Homeric ἐῴκειν (Od. 1.411). ἤικτο (Od. 20.31) beside ἔικτο (Il. 23.107) could represent earlier *ewewikto, a reduplicating aorist, as Schwyzer (1939:653 following Schulze 1966:305 n. 2 = KZ 43.185) holds, but could also be an unreduplicated pluperfect with long augment taken over from the active. But whatever the case with the pluperfect, certainly also to be connected with ἔοικα is Attic ἥκαζον (Ar. Ec. 385) ἥκασα (Ar. Nu. 350) to εἰκάζω 'portray, infer from comparison' which derives from *eeeika- > ἤεικα- > ἤκα-. But the precise constitution of the original form is uncertain. Frisk (1.452-453, 530) derives εἰκάζω from *wewika-, a factitive present built on the old intransitive perfect, and hence must hold that ἥκαζον derives from *e-wewika-. This supposition is possible, but is by no means inevitable. It seems to me to be in fact more likely that Sappho's ἐϊκάσδω (PLF 115) is artfully created by diektasis from εἰκάζω on the analogy of Homeric pluperfects like ἔϊκτην, and that it is not directly relevant to the history of εἰκάζω. If this form is removed from consideration, there is no longer any reason to favor derivation from *wewik-, a derivation which causes trouble with ἐπιεικής 'suitable, fitting' and εἰκών 'likeness, image'. Hence we can assume with some confidence that εἰκάζω < *weikadyo (to εἰκών ?), and that the ἠ- augment represents contraction of the ἐ- augment with the prothetic vowel in *əweik-, a prothetic vowel lost from the present tense.

5.5.2 Before discussing the exceptions to the rule: augment ἠ- is the contraction product of augment ἐ- plus prothetic vowel, it might be well to list those verbs with augment εἰ- (< *ewe-) in order to see whether they elsewhere display prothesis. εἴργω has been mentioned above.

ἐθίζω 'accustom' < *wedh- < *swedh- by dissimilation of aspiration (Frisk 1.449) has as its aorist εἴθισα (D. 20.68).

ἐλίττω (2.4.10 above), though suspected of containing prothesis, does not, and has the aorist εἴλιξα (Pl. *Ti.* 73a).

ἐρύω (2.4.11 above) again has been held to contain prothesis, and again does not. Its aorist is εἴρυσα (*Od.* 2.389, Hdt. 2.136).

ἑστιάω 'entertain', clearly a derivative of ἑστία 'hearth' (5.3.10 above) may have been created too late to be relevant. The aorist is εἱστίασα (Xen. *Cyn.* 1.3.10).

5.5.3 Problematic cases fall into two groups, those in which prothesis should occur but does not, and those in which it does occur but should not. In the first category belong only the two verbs εἶπον 'I said' and εἴκω 'yield' (5.3.2 above). And εἶπον is really no problem, for it is all but certain that it represents the contraction of *eweipon (cf. Schwyzer 1939:654), a form directly comparable with Skt. *avocam* < *ewewk^wom, an augmented reduplicating aorist (Frisk 1.464). Since unaugmented *weuk^wom (or dissimilated *weik^wom) would have developed prothesis (> *eweik^wom) and become homophonous with the augmented form, the prothetic vowel was dropped in non-finite forms and a regular *eweip- ~ *weip- relation established.

εἴκω is more of a problem, for its secondary tenses definitely show εἰ- (εἶκον *Il.* 16.305, εἶξα *Il.* 24.718). But because of the uncertainty of the etymology, it is possible to assume that the aorist is the earlier form (*ewiksa > εἶξα), and the primary tenses then formed to it. It is best, though, simply to leave εἴκω as an exception to the rule.

The three words which, counter to expectation, show a long augment are: ὁράω 'see' (< *worā — Frisk 2.409-410), ἄγνυμι 'break, shatter' (< *wag- ? — Frisk 1.13: etymology really unknown), and ἁλίσκομαι 'be taken, conquered' (< *wal-/*wel- Frisk 1.74: etymology really unknown).[45] All are problematic in that instead of showing ὠ- or ἠ- in the augmented tenses, they have ἑω, ἑᾱ-, ἑᾱ- respectively, forms which seem to be the metathesized results of earlier ἠο-, ἠα-, ἠα-. If this analysis, the usual one (Wackernagel 1953:583, Schwyzer 1939:653), is correct, then clearly we must assume a long augment ἠ-, an augment which appears where it should not.

But the long augment in these verbs may be more apparent than real, and may require explanation in another way. In the first place the phenomenon is Attic only: Ionic has ὤρα (Hdt. 1.11), ὤρηκα (Herod. 4.40); ἦξα (*Il.* 23.392), κατῆξα (Hp. *Epid.* 5.26); ἠλισκόμην (Hdt. 7.181), ἤλων (*Od.* 22.230, Hdt. 1.84). As a result we shall have to speak of a purely Attic ἠ- augment: contraction rather than metathesis as an explanation for the Ionic forms would create more problems than it would solve. Secondly, for whatever reason, long vowel forms appear also in unaugmented tenses of ἄγνυμι (κατᾱγῶ Ar. *Fr.* 604, κατᾱγείη Ar. *Ach.* 944, κατέᾱγα Ar. *Ach.* 1180; ἆξον *Il.* 6.306, ἆξαι *Il.* 21.178, ἐᾱγη *Il.* 11.559, ἑᾱγα Hes. *E.* 534) and ἁλίσκομαι (ἁλόντε *Il.* 5.487,

---

[45] There are a number of cases in which the long augment is perfectly regular. ἑώρταζον is the result of contraction and metathesis of *ewewortadzon; ἕᾱδον is metathesized from *hēwadon which in turn derives from *eswadon; ἑώικει comes from *ewewoikei; and ἑώργει is from *eweworgei. Two other cases which should be brought into the discussion at this point but rarely are, are: Attic ἑώθουν < ὠθέω and ἐωνούμην < ὠνέομαι, for both of which Ionic and epic (for ὠθέω) agree in not showing the ἑ-. The former presence of */w/- cannot explain the Attic forms, both because of the divergence between Attic and Ionic, and because */w/- was very early lost before /ɔ:/. We must assume rather that in Attic there obtained an optional rule: use syllabic augment in secondary tenses of verbs containing a long vowel in primary tenses. This rule seems to have operated only before ᾱ- and ω- (and οὐ in ἐούρουν D. 54.4), and to have been optional even there. It presumably arose as a result of the regular cases of metathesis listed above, and then spread to the others. The question then is, do ἁλίσκομαι, ὁράω, ἄγνυμι belong among cases of regular metathesis, or are they of analogical origin?

ἁλῶναι Hippon. 74 and in many forms of ἀναλίσκω), thus encouraging the feeling that the augment was ἐ-, but the stem of the verb āg- and hāl-. With ὁράω it seems that the perfect system operated on the imperfect (indeed ὁράω may have originally been perfective only — like οἶδα — and then either have been derived from the perfect or converted from a perfect into a present). In the perfect the long augment is perfectly regular: ἑόρᾱκα (Ar. *Th.* 32, 33), ἑωράκη (Pl. *Rep.* 328), (but ἑοράκεσαν — Thuc. 2.21) deriving from *weworāka and *eweworākea > *ēorakē > *ἑωράκη. Since the same relation existed in the imperfect stem, the notion arose that augmented tenses required lengthening of the vowel in the stem (this feeling accounts also for ἐῳνοχόει). Lengthening was regular in the pluperfect, analogical in the imperfect: ἑόρακα : ἑωράκη = ὁράω : ἑώρων. Hence other explanations than that of an augment ἠ- are, if not inevitable, at least possible.[46]

5.6.0 To sum up this section, then, we have tentatively arrived at three new conclusions concerning restrictions on the occurrence of prothesis. 1) -/sT/- is not to be included in -*RC*- (ἔσσα — 5.3.5, ἕσπερος, ἑστία — 5.3.10); this seems secure. 2) -/tr/- and -/kr/- are not to be included in -*CR*- (μέτρον — 5.2.2 and possibly νεκρός — 5.1.5), nor is -/ts/- (μέσος — 5.2.2). 3) -*RR*- seems not to occasion prothesis (λεῖος — 5.2.1, μεῖραξ, μείων, μέλλω — 5.2.2, νειός — 5.2.3, εἶλαρ — 5.3.3, εἶρος — 5.3.6, εἴρω — 5.3.7, ἕλμινς — 5.3.9), but because of numerous uncertainties this conclusion cannot yet be considered certain. For the rest, explanations — possibly, or rather probably, not all acceptable to all scholars — have been found for most words, thus en-

---

[46] The influence of the perfect (and pluperfect) may also have been exerted on *wal- and *wag- as well. Indeed *wal- in ἁλίσκομαι would seem almost certainly to be connected with εἰλέω, and originally to have meant something like 'be enclosed, boxed up', hence 'captured'. ἑάλων itself might well be a reformed perfect *wewaloya (cf. δείδω < *dedwoya) or pluperfect *ewewaloyea interpreted as an aorist and hence provided with -/n/. But I quite realize that my account of the origin of ἠ- in these problematic cases is unsatisfactory and in need of further discussion. I hope to be able to provide this further discussion in the none-too-distant future.

couraging us to assume that the rule for prothesis does indeed predict prothesis. The troublesome exceptions yet remaining are: λείχω, λέχριος — 5.2.1, νέφρος — 5.2.3, εἴκω — 5.3.2, not many, but enough to cast doubt on this assumption.

5.7.0 Next we may turn to instances of resonant followed by /a/-, a constellation of phonemes which will have been much rarer than Re- because /a/ is a rare IE phoneme. We have found only four words (ἐλαφρός — 2.1.4, ἐλάσσων — 2.1.5, ἀμαλδύνω — 2.2.5, *ἀμάργνυμι — 2.2.6) which indicate that prothesis develops before /a/. Hence strictly speaking only two environments — *laAˢᵖR- and *maLVᵈ- — are relevant. But as with *Re- I shall include all instances of *Ra- in a closed syllable.

5.7.1 The list of words the etymology of which is unknown is clearly a good deal longer here than was the case with *Re-. λαδρέω 'flow strongly' (2.71: unerklärt), λαίγματα· πέμματα, οἱ δὲ σπέρματα, ἱερὰ ἀπάργματα (Hsch.: 2.71: ohne Etymologie), λαιδρός 'bold, impudent' (2.72): though Frisk adduces a number of Baltic words this word is most likely not to be cognate with them. λαῖμα· τὸ ἱερόν (Hsch.: 2.71: ohne Etymologie), λαιμός 'throat' (2.72-73: keine brauchbare Anknüpfung), λαῖτμα 'depth (of the sea)' (2.74: isoliert), λαῖφος 'shabby garment' (2.74: unerklärt), λάμπη 'scum' beside λάπη (2.78: unerklärt), λαμπήνη 'covered chariot' (2.78), λάξ 'with the foot' (2.82-83: nicht sicher erklärt), λάπτω 'lap with the tongue' (2.85: onomatopoetic), λάρκος 'charcoal-basket' (2.86: nicht sicher erklärt), λάρναξ 'coffer' (2.86: < νάρναξ: weitere Analyse ganz unsicher), λάσθη 'mockery, insult' (2.87: ohne sichere Etymologie), λάτρον 'pay, hire' (2.89-90: eine überzeugende idg. Anknüpfung fehlt), λαυκανίη 'throat' (2.90-91: ohne sichere Entsprechung), Λαφρία, epithet of Artemis (2.91: unerklärt), μαίνη 'Maina vulgaris' (2.160: keine überzeugende Etymologie), μαίομαι 'seek after' (2.161-162: ohne überzeugende Entsprechung), μακκοάω 'be stupid' (2.164: dunkel), μακκούρα· χειρὶ σιδηρᾷ, ᾗ χρῶνται πρὸς τοὺς ἵππους (Hsch.: 2.164), μάλκη 'numbness from cold' (2.167-168: ohne überzeugende Erklärung), μαλλός 'flock of wool' (2.168: unerklärt), μάμμη 'mother' (2.168-169: Lallwort), μάνδαλος 'bolt'

(2.169: ohne Etymologie). μάνδρα 'enclosed space' (2.169), μανδραγόρας 'mandrake' (2.170: unerklärt), μάργος 'mad' (2.175: unerklärt), μάρπτω 'take hold of' (2.178: ohne aussergriechische Entsprechung), μασάομαι 'chew' (2.179-180), μάσθλης 'leather shoe' (2.180: Erklärung strittig), μάσταξ 'mouth, jaws' (2.182), μασχάλη 'arm-pit' (2.183-184: dunkel), μάτταβος· ὁ μωρός (Hsch.: 2.185), μάχλος 'lewd, lustful (of women)' (2.187: isoliert), μάψ 'in vain' (2.188: ohne sichere Erklärung), ναίω 'dwell' (2.286: < *nasyō: isoliert), ναός 'temple' (2.288: < *naswos to ναίω), νάρθηξ 'giant fennel' (2.289-290: dunkel), νάσσω (2.291: Etymologie unbekannt).

5.7.2 Despite the rarity of the phoneme /a/ in PIE, there do seem to be a few words which contained /a/ beginning with /s/. λάβρος 'furious' (2.66-67: to λαβεῖν), λάζομαι 'seize' (2.71), λαμβάνω 'take' (2.77-78), λάχνη 'down' (2.93), μάρτυς 'witness' (2.178-179), νάρκη 'numbness' (2.290), νάρκισσος 'narcissus' (2.290-291), ἀνδάνω 'please' (1.104).

5.7.3 Clearly many of the Grk. words containing Ra- are borrowed. λαβρώνιον 'large wide cup' (2.67: Fremdwort ?), λαισήϊα 'shield' (2.74: Fremdwort), λάκκος 'kind of garment' (2.76: from Prakrit lakkha 'lacquer'), λακχά, plant name = ἄγχουσα (2.76: Fremdwort), λάρδος 'salted meat' (2.85: from Lat. lardum), μάγδωλος 'watch-tower' (2.155-156: aus dem Semit.), μάδρυα = κοκκύμηλα 'plums' (2.158: wohl Fremdwort), μανδάκης 'truss' (2.169: thrakisches LW), μανδύα 'woolen cloak' (2.170: unerklärtes Fremdwort), μαντία 'blackberry' (1.226 s.v. βάτος: Mittelmeerwort), μαργαρίτης 'pearl' (2.174-175: orientalisches LW), μάρσιππος 'bag, pouch' (2.178: Fremdwort), μαρτιχόρας 'man-eater', i.e. 'tiger' (2.178: aus dem Iranischen), μαῦλις 'bawd' (2.186: von lyd. *mav-lis), νάβλα 'musical instrument' (2.285: phönikisch), νάρδος 'spikenard' (2.289: aus dem Semit.), ναῦσσον, name of a tax (2.294: Karisches Fremdwort), νάφθα 'naphtha' (2.294: Aus npers. naft 'asphalt, petroleum').

5.7.4 A number of words, though possibly IE, are not relevant to the rule because they did not exist in PGrk. in a shape subject to the rule. λαίθαργος 'biting secretly' (2.72: deformation of λήθαργος), λαικάζω 'wench' (2.72: a variant of ληκάω), λαῖλαψ 'furious storm' (2.72: intensive reduplication: sonst isoliert), λαινό-χειρ· σκληρόχειρ (Hsch.: 2.73: < λάϊνος 'stony' to λᾶας), λαιός, kind of thrush (2.74: probably from λᾶας 'stone'), λαιφάσσω 'swallow greedily' (2.74: blend of λαιμάσσω + λαφύσσω), λαι-ψηρός 'swift' (2.74: expressive Umbildung von αἰψηρός), λάμπω 'shine' (2.79-80): all IE cognates show a root *lāp ~ *lap, so the Grk. nasal is an innovation. λανθάνω 'escape notice' (2:80-82); the basic forms of the paradigm are *lāth- ~ *lath-: again the nasal present is a Grk. innovation. λάσκω 'ring': λάσκω (< *lakskō) is secondary to the aorist λακεῖν (2.88-89: ohne sichere ausser-griechische Entsprechung), λάσται· πόρναι (Hsch.: 2.89: to λιλαί-ομαι), λατμενεία· δουλεία (Hsch.: 2.89: from ἀτμενία and λατρεία), μαγδαλιά 'inside of the loaf' (2.155: late for ἀπομαγδαλιά), μαιμάω 'be very eager' (2.159-160: reduplicated intensive either to μαίομαι or μῶμαι 'seek after'), μανθάνω 'learn' (2.170-171): again the present is secondary, and all Grk. forms derive from μαθεῖν. μαρμαίρω 'flash' (2.176: intensive reduplication to the root *mar-), ναύκληρος 'shipowner' (2.291-292) and numerous other derivatives of nau- (2.292-294).

5.7.5 A number of the words listed in the above category might well have been listed here among words with prothesis ana-logically lost, words like μανθάνω λανθάνω and the intensive reduplications like λαῖλαψ and μαιμάω. And indeed it is difficult to find candidates for this category unless the above are included. μαίνομαι 'rage' (2.160-161) < *manyomai could lack the pro-thetic vowel because of the aorist μανῆναι, or because the internal cluster is a member of -RR-. μάντις 'diviner' (2.172-173) could then in turn be analogical to μαίνομαι. μάρμαρος 'crystalline rock' (2.176-177), if from μάρναμαι, could have its initial after the non-prothetic verb. μᾶζα 'barley-cake' (2.158-159) could have its initial after μάσσω. And μάσσω 'knead' may well have failed to develop prothesis because of the analogy of the aorist μαγῆναι, a word which contains the only form of the stem (*mag-) attested to in other IE languages (2.180-181).

5.7.6 In spite of all the borrowings and late creations, there is nonetheless a troublesome residue. λαῖον (only in A. R. 3.1335), if connected with Skt. *lunắti* 'cut' and *lavί-* 'sickle' (Frisk 2.73). But there are phonological difficulties, and this connection seems unlikely. λαιός 'left' < *laiwos*, cognate with Lat. *laevus* (2.73), λάκκος 'pond' < *lakwos* to Lat. *lacus* (2.75-76), λαύρα 'alley, lane' (2.91: to λᾶας?), μάγγανον 'philtre, iron peg' (2.155), but cf. μάνδαλος 'iron peg' (2.169), of which *mang-* may be a variant, a relation which points rather to a borrowing into Grk. and hence suggests that these words should both be included in 5.7.1. μαζός, μασθός, μαστός 'breast' (2.183), but the etymology is really unknown. Is Ἀμαζών (= [amazdo:n]) *μαζών with prothesis? If so, the word makes some sense: 'breasted (warriors)'. μακρός 'long' (2.164-165) has -/TR/-, and μάσσων 'longer' (2.224-225) does not contain prothesis either because it contained -/ky/- or by analogy with μακρός. Μαῖρα, name of the dog-star (2.176 s.v. μαρμαίρω). μαλθακός 'soft' (2.167) has beside it the Aeolic μόλθακος (Alcaeus *PLF* A 6.9, Z 14.8), and this may be the more original form. μόρναμαι 'fight' (2.177-178) beside βάρναμαι (1.221) shows that *mranamai* < *mrnamai* was the original form. Or was it *mornamai* > *marnamai*? ματτύη, a rich, highly flavored dessert (2.185-186). ναί 'yea, verily' (2.286) has beside it also the form νή. ναί is probably secondary: cf. the interchange of αι and η in 5.7.4. ἄγνυμι 'break' (1.13) may be secondary to the perfect (cf. n. 46). Otherwise it is an exception. αἴνω 'sift, winnow' (1.41) < *wanyo. ἀΐσσω 'shoot, dart' (1.45-46) if, as seems most likely, it derives from *waiwikyo. But perhaps, since the word is an intensive reduplication, it did not exist in PGrk. times and hence is to be included in 5.7.4. ἄστυ 'town' (1.173-174) is no problem since -/st/- does not allow prothesis. What is surprising is that aspiration did not develop, thus leading to *ἅστυ. More on this below (6.3).

5.7.7 The troublesome residue here is really not very troublesome, for most possibly difficult cases can be accounted for in other ways. The only words that might conceivably worry my position are λαύρα, μαλθακός and ἄγνυμι. Indeed prothesis is so rare before

Ra-, and the opportunities for its arising so few, that we cannot even derive support from 5.7.6 for the nonoccurrence of prothesis before *-CC-* (λάκκος, ματτύη) and further confirmation for the fact that prothesis does not occur before syllables closed (or at least terminated) by *-TR-* (μακρός). Most cases of Grk. /a/ are not inherited, but developed in Grk. from the vocalization of the sonant liquids and nasals, and indeed the only cases we have thus far seen of prothesis before *Ra-* have in fact shown /a/ < */n/ (ἐλαφρός ἐλάσσων), < /r/ (*ἀμάργνυμι) and < /l/ (ἀμαλδύνω). For the present at least all we are justified in concluding from this section is that prothesis is rare before *Ra-*. This fact may be due to the further fact that *Ra-* is rare and hence be of statistical interest only; or it may be that *Ra-* in some way resisted the development of prothesis, in which event the absence of prothesis is significant.

5.8.0 The words just discussed and the occurrence (or rather non-occurrence) of prothesis before *Ra-* might lead one to deny that prothesis ever occurred before the low central vowel: we can, after all invoke analogy to account for the actually occurring instances. Not so with /i/. There are only four cases of prothesis before *Ra-* (or five, if we include Ἀμαζών — 5.7.6), but there are four cases, sure cases, of prothesis before /i/: ἀλίνειν (2.1.3), ὀμίχλη (2.2.4), ἔικοσι (2.4.2), ἔίση (2.4.6); three cases in which prothesis is highly likely: ὀλιβρόν ὀλισθάνω (3.1.11), ἐνιπή (3.3.4), ἔίσομαι (5.3.8); ἀίω (4.4.4) and ὀίω (4.4.5) are relatively unlikely, while there is uncertainty concerning the vocalic nucleus of ὀλ(ε)ίζων (2.1.7): it is best kept separate. The remarkable thing about the above list of nine instances is that /i:/ figures in five certain cases and may figure in two more: only in ὀμίχλη and ὀλιβρόν ὀλισθάνω have we no reason to suppose /i:/, and with them the influence of /ei/ is possible. For this reason and because all syllables capable of producing prothesis have thus far been closed, we have been led to analyze /i:/ as /iy/. If this analysis is accepted, then we can state that the environments in which /i/ admits prothesis are: *RiyC-* and $RiC\begin{bmatrix}l\\r\end{bmatrix}$- (ὀλισθάνω still remaining problematic). These, then are the only truly critical

environments. Nonetheless, as before, I shall include all cases of
*RiCC -.

5.8.1 Words of the proper shape, but of uncertain etymology, and
hence most likely non-IE, include: λιγνύς 'thick smoke mixed
with flame' (2.121: unerklärt), λίμβος = λίχνος (Hsch.: 2.124:
unerklärt), λῑμός 'hunger' (2.124-125: ohne aussergriechische
Entsprechung), λιμφός· συκοφάντης ἢ μηνύτης παρανόμων (Hsch.:
2.125: unerklärt), λίπτομαι 'be eager' (2.127-128), λῑπαρέω 'be-
seech' (2.127-128): though many cognates are mentioned, none is
convincing. λῑρός 'bold, lewd' (2.128: nicht sicher erklärt), λίς
'smooth', λῑτός 'simple', λισσός 'smooth' (2.128-129): there seem
to be no extra-Greek cognates. λίσγος in λισγάριον 'spade,
mattock' (2.129: nicht sicher erklärt), λίσπος 'smooth' (2.129:
probably connected with λισσός), λισσάνιος, form of address
(2.129-130: ohne sichere Etymologie), λίστρον 'tool for leveling'
(2.130: ohne sichere Erklärung), λιψουρία 'desire to make water'
(2.131: to λίπτω), μιλλός· βραδύς, χαῦνος (Hsch.: 2.237: unerklärt),
μίλφοι 'falling off of the eyelashes' (2.238: etymologisch dunkel),
μίνθος 'human ordure' (2.242: dunkel), μιργάβωρ· τὸ λυκόφως,
μιργῶσαι· πηλῶσαι (Hsch.: 2.243): Frisk mentions etymological
connection with Lith. mirgěti 'glimmer', but this seems unlikely.
μῑσέω 'hate' (2.243-244: eine überzeugende Etymologie ... nicht
gefunden), μιστύλλω 'cut up' (2.244-245): a number of connections have been suggested, all uncertain. μίσχος 'stalk' (2.245:
ohne Etymologie), νίκη 'victory' (2.320-321: eine überzeugende
Etymologie fehlt), ἴλια· μόρια γυναικεῖα; ἴλιον· τὸ τῆς γυναικὸς
ἐφήβαιον δηλοῖ. καὶ κόσμον γυναικεῖον παρὰ Κῴοις (Hsch.: 1.722).
Many possibilities have been suggested, but none convinces.

5.8.2 Words in which an initial */s/- has been suspected. λίγδην
'grazing', λίζω 'graze' (2.121), μικρός 'small' (2.237), μῖλαξ 'holm-
oak' (2.237, 749), ἰδίω 'sweat' ἶδος 'sweat' (1.709-710), ἱδρώς
'sweat' (1.710-711).

5.8.3 A number of words are suspect of being loans. λίνδος, an
aromatic plant (2.125), probably the same word as the city name
Λίνδος. λίς 'lion' (2.113: same as Hebrew lajiš 'lion'), λίτρα, silver

coin of Sicily (2.131: Mittelmeerwort), μίλτος 'red earth' (2.237-238: technisches Fremdwort), μῖμος 'imitator' (2.241: because of its technical meaning probably a loan-word), μίνθα 'mint' (2.241-242: Fremdwort), μίτρα 'waist-guard' (2.246: Entlehnung, vielleicht aus indoiranischer Quelle), νίτρον 'sodium carbonate' (2.321: orient. LW), ἰξός 'oak-misteltoe' (1.728-729: altes Kulturwort), ἴον 'violet' (1.729: aus einer Mittelmeersprache entlehnt).

5.8.4 The following words most likely derive from roots present in PGrk., but were formed to these roots later on. λιμπάνω 'leave' (2.99-100 and above 5.1.4), merely a different present formed to the PGrk. aoristic λιπεῖν. λίσσομαι 'beg' (2.130), secondary to λιτή λιτέσθαι. μείγνυμι or μίγνυμι 'mix' (2.192-193 and above 5.1.4) seems clearly a secondary formation to the aorist μιγῆναι, and then subsequently μεῖξαι. μίσγω < *migskō. μιστύλη 'piece of bread scooped out as a spoon' (2.278), a later form from earlier and original μυστίλη. ἴσκω 'make like' = ἐΐσκω (1.737) is almost certainly a poetic shortening of ἐΐσκω on the model of ἶσος : ἐΐση.

5.8.5 There seem to be no cases of words with prothesis lost before Ri-. But again it may well be that a number of the recalcitrant cases of wi- belong here.

5.8.6 The troublesome residue includes:

λιβρός = σκοτεινός καὶ μέλας (Hp. apud Erot.) beside λιμβρός (EM 564.52). Frisk (2.120-121) assumes connection with λείβω, but the word is too rare and of too uncertain semantic interpretation to count for much.

λικμάω 'winnow' (2.122-123). The initial of this word and the medial cluster vary so much that we must conclude that a foreign word is here being adapted to Grk.

μισθός 'hire' (2.244) has -/sth/-.

νίζω 'wash' with its many derivatives comes from *nigʷyo (2.319-320). This has to be reckoned a problematic case.

ἰδνόομαι 'bend oneself double' (1.710). This word is included here because Frisk finds IE cognates, but it is almost certainly a popular word with no IE ancestry.

ἵεμαι 'hasten' (1.711). Prothesis develops only in closed syllables, as it did in the future and aorist of this verb (5.3.8 above).

ἱέραξ 'hawk' (1.712). Frisk assumes an original *wīros, but this is unnecessary, and leads to complicated explanations.

ἴκελος (and εἴκελος) 'like' (1.716) may be the non-prothetic and the prothetic forms respectively of *wi:k- ∼ *wik-.

ἴλη 'band, troop' (1.722) is difficult to explain, but seems best taken with Frisk from *wiwla.

ἱμάτιον (Ion. εἱμάτιον) 'outer garment' is connected with the root *wes-, (1.725), and hence does not allow prothesis (5.3.5).

ἴμβω-ἴμψας· ζεύξας. Θετταλοί (Hsch.). γιμβάναι· ζεύγανα (Hsch.: 1.725-726).

ἰός 'poison' (1.730) has /i:/, but not in a closed syllable.

Ἶρις, messenger of the gods, (1.735), in spite of Frisk's attempts, is probably non-IE.

ἴς, ἰνός 'sinew, strength' (1.735-736) seems an exception to the rule.

ἱστία 'hearth' (1.576-577) is a by-form of the more regular ἑστία, and is prevented from developing prothesis by the -/s/- (5.3.10

ἵστωρ 'judge' (1.740-741) likewise fails to develop a prothetic vowel, though other words of the same root did (ἀείδω 3.4.2 and ἤειδη 5.5.1). ἰσχύς 'strength' (1.742-743) is still another example of aspiration rather than prothesis before -/s/- (below 6.3.1). ἰτέα 'willow' (1.743) may be an exception, but is just as likely not to be an IE word.

5.8.7 Of the above seeming exceptions ἰδνόομαι ἵμβω Ἶρις ἰτέα (unless it should represent εἰτέα < *ewītea) λιβρός are most likely non-IE; ἵεμαι ἱέραξ ἰός are not relevant because the */iy/ was not in a closed syllable; λικμάω ἴλη (if < *wiwla) ἱστία ἵστωρ μισθός do not have the proper internal cluster; and ἱμάτιον is clearly modeled or remodeled on ἕννυμι. There remain, then, only: νίζω, but there also exists χέρνιψ 'water for washing the hands', thus indicating that this word might belong in 5.8.5; ἴς ἰνός is the only remaining problematic case. We may conclude that none of these troublesome exceptions is serious enough to invalidate the rule.

5.9.0 It has been useful to examine these many words because we have been able to isolate certain clusters that do not allow prothesis, and have thereby been able to be more specific in our formulation of the rule. And the more accurate formulation encourages us the more to feel that the rule is correct. There are four restrictions: 1) prothesis does not occur when the syllable following the resonant is closed by /s/ plus a consonant (5.6.0 and elsewhere): /s/ is not to be included in *R-; 2) syllables closed by -/tr/-, -/ts/- (5.6.0) and by -/kr/- (5.7.7 — ?) do not develop prothesis; 3) -RR- is not a member of -CR- or of -RC- (5.6.0 and elsewhere): the classes -R- and -C- are mutually exclusive, a fact which accounts also for 4): -CC- is not a member of -RC- or -CR-, a conclusion drawn hesitantly from the words found in 5.7.7 above.

5.9.1 It seems that there are further restrictions in the case of -CR-, and that we can be more specific in our formulation. If we exclude ὀλείζων (2.1.7) because the syllable originally contained /ei/ and not /i/; and ὀλόπτειν (2.1.8) because the vowel is not likely to be prothetic, then we find that most cases of -CR- contain an aspirate: ἐλαφρός (2.1.4) ἐλάττων < *elak^{h}yōn (2.1.5) ὀμίχλη (2.2.4) ἄεθλος (3.4.1) ἄθρις (5.3.1). The exceptions to this observation are ἀνεψιός (2.3.2) in which the ἀ- might be copulative; or failing that, one stage in the passage of */pti/ > */psi/ might have been something like *[p^{h}t^{h}i]; or /psi/ might in fact, as Attic spelling would indicate, have been /p^{h}si/. ἔεδνον is an artificial case of prothesis resulting from an incorrect analysis of ἀνάεδνον as ἀν + ἄεδνον > ἔεδνον (above 2.4.1). ὀλιβρόν and ὀλισθάνω as always are exceptions, but will be fit into the picture in the next chapter. And, since the only resonants to occur in the above list of cases containing -CR- are /r l y/, we can be more specific in our formulation, and schematically show:

$$*R\begin{bmatrix}e\\a\\i\end{bmatrix}A^{sp}\begin{bmatrix}r\\l\\y\end{bmatrix}- \quad > \quad *əR\begin{bmatrix}e\\a\\i\end{bmatrix}A^{sp}\begin{bmatrix}r\\l\\y\end{bmatrix}-$$

The only possible exceptions now remaining are λέχριος νεφρός (both 5.2.1 above). νεβρός (5.2.1) ἄγνυμι (5.7.6) νίζω (5.8.6) are no longer exceptions because of the narrower formulation of the rule.

5.9.2 One might infer from the above that there are restrictions also on -RC-, but in fact there seem to be none, at least on -R-. The class -R- includes all the resonants /r l m n w y/, though */m/ happens not to be represented, which is merely to say that a nasal does not appear before a labial stop; and there are only two cases of */n/: ἄημι (4.4.3) with the prothesis from ἀέντες etc., and ἐνεγκεῖν (3.3.3). Because of ἐέρση (2.4.5) ἐέλσαι (2.4.8) εἴσομαι (5.3.8) ἐλεύσομαι (3.1.9) we must include /s/ in -C-.[47] Though voiceless stops and the nasal /n/ rarely occur, they do occur often enough to discourage us from excluding them from -C-: /n/ is the only resonant to be included also in -C-. Only */r/ and */u/ do not admit voiceless stops, occurring as they do before /s/: ἐέρση (2.4.5), ἐλεύσομαι (3.1.9); Asp: ἔνερθεν (2.3.3), ἐλεύθερος (2.1.6): and voiced stops: ἐέργω (2.4.3), ἐργάζομαι (5.5.1). We will return to this restriction on /r/ below, but for the present we can remain satisfied with the rule:

$$*R\begin{bmatrix}e\\a\\i\end{bmatrix}RC- \quad > \quad *\partial R\begin{bmatrix}e\\a\\i\end{bmatrix}RC-$$

The only troublesome exceptions now remaining are λείβω λείχω both from 5.2.1 above, μαλθακός (5.2.6) and εἴκω (5.3.2). λευκός (5.2.1) and λαύρα (5.2.6) need not be considered exceptions if we accept the restriction placed on prothesis before syllables closed by /u/ just mentioned.

---

[47] It is worth noting, though, that these /s/'s differ from ordinary IE */s/ in that they do not disappear intervocalically and do not disappear (after /l/ and /r/) with compensatory lengthening of the preceding syllable.

THE REASONS FOR PROTHESIS

6.0 With the rule for the occurrence of prothesis securely formulated, we must now pass to a consideration of the reasons why
a prothetic vowel developed. In fact there is only one reason and
that a fairly simple one. Since prothesis is an anticipation (or
underlining) of voicing present in initial resonants, and since
voicing ordinarily is an automatic (hence non-distinctive) feature
of such resonants, there can have been no prothesis in Grk.
without there at the same time having existed initial resonants
lacking voice. That is to say that, in order for voicing in resonants
to be distinctive, it had also to be contrastive: certain resonants
had to be positively voiced in certain environments, not simply
redundantly so. We may take as a paradigm of this statement
developments involving the IE resonant */r/- in Grk. It is of
course well known that PIE */r/- in initial position appears in
historical Grk. times either as [hr] or as /er/ ∼ /or/. And [hr]
develops from earlier */sr/- (ῥέω < *srewō — Frisk 2.650-652)
and */wr/- (ῥήγνυμι < *wrēg- — Frisk 2.652-653), while /er/ ∼
/or/ continues PIE initial */r/- (ἐρυθρός < *rudh- — Frisk
1.567-568). It seems altogether most likely that it was the opposition /hr/- (< */sr/- and */wr/-) ≠ */r/- that caused the
voicing present in */r/- to be perceived as distinctive, and hence
to be underlined or strengthened by developing a separate vowel,
thus giving */hr/- ≠ */Vr/-. Put another way: the opposition
voiceless [r̥]: voiced [r] was factored into [hr] ≠ [Vr] by assigning
voicelessness to [h] and voice to [V]. (The superscript circle
indicates voicelessness in resonants.) This explanation brings with
it also a relative chronology, for it is clear that [hr] ([r̥]) must
have developed before prothesis could, for prothesis results precisely from the opposition */hr/- ≠ */r/-, hence:

1) $\begin{bmatrix} \text{sr-} \\ \text{wr-} \end{bmatrix}$ > /hr/-

2) /r/- > /ər/-

It is my contention that these rules, or a variety of them, account also for prothesis before the other resonants. The rules will be phrased somewhat differently, though, since */sR/- and */wR/-[48] do not figure here to the same extent. The rules will read:

1) /R/- > [R]/__$\begin{bmatrix} e \\ a \\ i \end{bmatrix}$RC-

[R̥] elsewhere

2) [R] > [əR]-

Thus, for instance, taking two words containing the same initial segment *mel-, μέλω 'be an object of care or thought' and ἀμέλγω 'milk' (2.2.2), and applying the rules to them, we get:

1) *mel- > *mel- /__g

> *m̥el- /__Vowel

2) *melg- > *əmelg-

6.1.1 But it is clear that the second change as presented is unmotivated because the alternation voiced-voiceless is automatic both in terms of the following vowel and of the syllable coda: all */m/- before /eRC/ are voiced (> *[əm]), while */m/- in all

---

[48] Possibly only */sr/- is to be invoked, for Mycenaean is thought to preserve initial */wr/- intact, and yet shows prothesis before /r/-. Thus we find: wi-ri-za 'root' (?) KN Od M 26 (Chadwick 1963:242), wi-ri-no 'hide' PY Ub 1318, wi-ri-ni-jo KN 'of hide' (Chadwick ibid.), o-u-ru-to (= hō wruntoi) 'thus they are guarding' PY An 657 (Chadwick 1963:243), beside ra-pte 'tailor' PY An 172 (Chadwick 1963:241-242) and ri-jo, name of a costal town (= ῾Ρίον: Chadwick 1963:243). Yet at the same time we find e-ru-ta-ra 'red' MY Ge 602 (Chadwick 1963:194). It is best, therefore, at least at present, to omit */wr/- and assume only */sr/- in the argument. The reasons for assuming an early merger of */sr/- (*/hr/?) and */wr/- appear below in n. 55.

other environments is voiceless. Hence, in order for the contrast between [m̥] and [m] to have been perceived, there must have intervened a rule (or rules) between rules 1) and 2) which destroyed the automatic nature of the alternation and rendered the contrast between [m̥] and [m] distinctive. It seems that this rule will be the same rule which applied with */r/-, namely the passage of initial */s/- to */h/- before resonants, thus giving rise to initial clusters */hR/-. Hence we need the rule:

   a)   */s/-   >   */h/- /__R-

which is in all probability merely a small part of the larger rule */s/ > */h/. But it it is clear that *[hR] must have merged with [R̥] in the new phonemic cluster */hR/-: otherwise the contrast between [R] and [R̥] would have yet remained automatic. Hence we need the rule:

   b) $\begin{bmatrix} [R̥] \\ [hR] \end{bmatrix}$-   >   /hR/-

6.1.2 There is a principled reason for assuming that [R̥] and [hR] merged in */hR/- and not in */R̥/-. We have supposed provisionally above (3.1.11) that *sleidh- lies behind ὀλισθάνω, and that the connection between the two words is to be made by assuming the development: *sleidh- > *hleidh- > *leidh- > *əleidh- > *oleidh-. And to the aorist ὄλισθε of this *oleidh-, or possibly to the aorist passive ὀλίσθην, there could easily have been formed a secondary present ὀλισθάνω. This still seems the best explanation, though it does of course require the assumption of several forms of this root no longer attested in Grk. But whatever the precise development, it is abundantly clear that, given the rules we have heretofore established, for ὀλισθάνω to have a prothetic vowel, it must have had a distinctively voiced initial */l/-. For this to have happened, */hl/- must have been dissimilated by following aspiration to */l/ (and not to /l̥/). Thus we need a rule which dissimilates initial aspiration and replaces initial */hR/- with */R/-.

   Now the observation made in 5.9.1 above concerning the restriction of -CR- to -AspR- finds its explanation, as does the reason for assuming [R̥] > /hR/. ἐλαφρός and all other such forms containing -*CR*- were affected by rules 1) and b), and hence passed through the stages: *$lap^{h}rós$ > *$l\overset{\circ}{a}p^{h}rós$ > *$hlap^{h}rós$. They would not have been subject to rule 2) and have developed prothesis, for prothesis develops only before initial voiced resonants, had they not also been affected by rule c) as well:

c) */hR/- > /R/- /__VAspR

a rule which causes aspiration of an initial resonant to disappear when that resonant appears in a syllable closed by aspiration. The reason for phrasing the rule in this way with its restriction to closed syllables is two-fold: on the one hand prothesis occurs only when the second aspirate is followed by a resonant, and on the other there are many words (such as λέχος 'bed' and μέθυ 'wine') in which prothesis does not occur and where it should if *lek^{h}os with voiced [l]- (rather than *l$\overset{\circ}{e}k^{h}os$) were subject to rule 2). We can get around this difficulty by assuming that, though all initial aspirated resonants lost their aspiration before following aspiration, prothesis developed only in a syllable closed by an aspirate or a resonant.[49] Whether or not this particular solution is adopted, it is at least clear either that *hleidh- first passed to *leidh- by dissimilation of aspirates, at which time it fell in with other *leid- and hence developed prothesis; or that *hlidh- passed to *lidh-, which form, when followed by *R*, fell in with *lap^{h}ros, etc., and passed to ϴlidh-. The reason that νείφω did not develop in this way is that it is a later replacement for earlier *niph- (5.1.2), and that *nip^{h}- never was followed by *R*. An approximation to the order and form of the rules follows:

1) [R]- > [R̥]- save in /__ $\begin{bmatrix} e \\ a \\ i \end{bmatrix}$ RC-

2) /s/- > /h/-

[49] The only possible objection I can think of to this formulation is that it would create *nip^{h}a from *snip^{h}a too early, presumably at a time prior to the creation of the compound ἀγάννιφος, and hence render this form inexplicable. Lengthening before resonants in Homer (Chantraine 1948:176-177) seems to require that *hl- still have been present at least during the early stages of the oral epic tradition in cases like: ὄρεα νιφόεντα (*Od.* 19.338) and ἰδέ λόφον (*Il.* 6.469).

3)   [R̥]-   >   /hR/-

4)   /hR/-   >   /R/ /__/Asp/

5)   /R/-   >   /əR/ /__$\begin{bmatrix} e \\ a \\ i \end{bmatrix}\begin{bmatrix} RC \\ AspR \end{bmatrix}$

6.1.3 This relative chronology requires expansion and elaboration. It is abundantly clear by now that the first environment I have isolated is in part merely the residue remaining after the application of a rule of wider extent which devoiced initial resonants save when in a syllable closed by a resonant. Hence the environment I have isolated merely provides a restriction on the application of the rule. The environment -$\begin{bmatrix} e \\ a \\ i \end{bmatrix}$Asp- is a positive one, though, providing some of the input to rule 5). That rules 2), 3) and 4) follow each other in that order will not be doubted by anyone (unless they feel that 1) and 3) should be collapsed into a single rule), but that they follow rule 1) is dictated not by any practical necessity, but by one (to me) rather important theoretical consideration. It seems unlikely that prothesis would have developed as it did if rule 1) followed rule 4), though nothing would be changed in the results. For we have supposed that there developed an allophonic relation in initial resonants whereby resonants were voiceless in certain predictable environments and voiced in others. This alternation was completely automatic and hence imperceptible to speakers of PGrk. Something changed the automatic nature of the alternation, and that something must have been rules 2) and 3). Hence 1) must precede. But of course this line of argument is merely a repetition of what has been said before, and must be turned around. If */sR/- > */hR/- preceded rule 1), it seems unlikely that rule 1) would have applied at all, for there would already have existed a non-automatic opposition between initial aspirated resonants and initial voiced resonants. And the distinction, if any, between [R̥] and [hR] is so slight that the previous existence of /hR/- would probably have been enough to prevent the passage of [R] to [R̥] in those environments in which it did take place. Lest it be objected that by the same line of argument */sR/- should have been prevented from passing to /hR/- by the previous existence of [R̥], it will be recalled that */sR/- > */hR/- (rule 2) is merely a part of the larger rule: */s/ > /h/, and it is therefore essentially accidental that there already existed an [R̥] with which [hR] could merge. Nonetheless the rules work equally well with rule 1) first or fourth, so that if the above argumentation should prove unpalatable, one may choose whichever order one prefers. That rule 5) completes the series seems obvious to me, but other positions for 5) may be possible.

This formulation and chronology will perhaps require modification later on, but we may for the moment at least allow it to stand, and indeed will find that it works unconditionally for /m n l/. But we must also include in these rules the semivowels /r w y/. It will be best to treat them individually first, setting up the rules governing each sound, and then attempt to bring all the rules together at the end and combine them with those of 6.1.2 into a final formulation.

6.2.0 Initial /r/ in Class. Grk. is always [hr] and derives from */sr/- and */wr/-. All other cases of PIE */r/- in Grk. develop a prothetic vowel and appear as ἀρ- ἐρ- ὀρ-, or so the handbooks say (Schwyzer 1939:411, Lejeune 1955:127). And if these handbook statements should be correct, then we need only the rules given in 6.0 above:

a) $\begin{bmatrix} sr \\ wr \end{bmatrix}$ > [hr]

b) [r] > [ər]

expressed in this order. But there are several words with [hr]-which have sometimes been suspected to contain IE */r/-, and they must be discussed before we can accept the rule as being valid in the way formulated. ῥέζω 'dye' together with its various derivatives (LSJ s. ῥέζω) has been compared with Skt. *rájyati* 'sich färben', *rāga-* 'Färben' (Frisk 2.647-648, Lejeune 1955:127), and if this connection is accepted, the rule will require rephrasing. Likewise ῥυκάνη 'plane' (Lejeune *ibid.*), if connected with Lat. *runcare* 'weed', constitutes another exception, but the connection seems rather unlikely (Frisk 2.665). And, as Frisk says (2.666-667), ῥυσός 'shriveled, wrinkled' may have only a chance similarity with Lat. *ruga* 'wrinkle' and Lith. *raũkas* 'id.'. ῥώομαι 'move with speed' beside ἐρωή 'quick motion' (Lejeune *ibid.*), has no good etymology (Frisk 2.668), but would seem to be a case of non-prothetic */r/-. ῥαίω 'break, shatter' has frequently been connected with Skt. *risyati* 'Schaden nehmen' in spite of the absence of prothesis, but Frisk (2.640), stressing that the -*s*- of ῥαισθῆναι can be analogical, assumes that ῥαίω is a Reimwort to the semantically similar παίω πταίω. Nonetheless this word cannot be excluded from consideration out of hand. Hence the prothesis rule for */r/- as usually formulated may not be sufficient.

6.2.1 Not only is it possible that the rule fails to account for forms without prothesis, it is furthermore remarkable that several of the cases of prothesis before */r/- listed by Schwyzer and Lejeune, in addition to obeying the rule in 6.2.0, obey also the rules of 6.1.2.

ἐρεύγομαι (S. L.) 'belch out, bellow' (Frisk 1.554-555) is cognate with Lat. *ērūgo* and *rūgio*.

ἐρεύθω (S.) 'make red' (Frisk 1.555) is cognate with ON *rjōða* 'blutig machen' and numerous Lat. and Skt. forms. Schwyzer also includes here ἐρυθρός 'red' which without a doubt is connected with Skt. *rudhira*- and Lat. *ruber* 'red', and also without a doubt contains a prothetic vowel. This vowel can either have developed independently before **rudh*-, or can have been extended to it by analogy with ἐρεύθω. Both these words obey rules 1) and 5), as do:

ἐρείδω 'prop, support', if connected with Latin *ridica* 'stake', (Frisk 1.551);

ἐρείκω 'rend, bruise', if connected with Skt. *rikháti* 'ritzen', Lith. *riekiù, riẽkti* 'Brot schneiden' (Frisk 1.551-552);

ἐρείπω 'throw down', if connected with ON *rīfa* 'zerreissen' and Lat. *rīpa* 'bank' (Frisk 1.552);

if we should want to include them here. Since the above cases conform to the rules for prothesis established for /l m n w/, it might be well to go through the other cases of prothesis listed by Schwyzer and Lejeune to see whether possibly the prothesis rule for */r/- has not been unjustifiably generalized in the past.

Ἔρεβος (L.S.) 'Erebus, a place of nether darkness, forming a passage from Earth to Hades', occurring first in the *Iliad* (16. 327), has always been compared with Skt. *rájas-* 'dunkler Luftkreis', Arm. *erek* 'Abend', Goth. *riqiz* 'Dunkel', and derived from an IE *reg^wos- (n. Frisk 1.550). There seems no reason to call this etymology into question.

ἐρέφω (L.S.) 'cover with a roof' (*Il.* +), though almost certainly of IE origin (Frisk 1.556), has few IE cognates. The best of these is OHG *hirni-reba* 'Schädel' (eig. 'Hirnbedeckung') according to Frisk, and Russ. *rebró* 'rib'. Prothesis does seem the best explanation, at least until a better comes along, in spite of the lack of good cognates. Schwyzer also includes ὄροφος 'roof', but this form is most likely to be analogical after ἐρέφω, coming from *rop^hos > *$erop^hos$ > ὄροφος.

ἀρήγω (L.S.) 'aid, succour' (*Il.*+) is generally connected with OHG *geruohhen*, OSax. *rōkjan* 'Sorge tragen' (Frisk 1.137, Chantraine 1968:107), though without any overwhelming degree of confidence. Still more questionable is connection with Lat. *regō* 'guide' and Grk. ὀρέγω, as well as with Skt. *rájā-* 'king'. This example had best be considered hypothetical, and to be included only if the rules to be formulated later allow it.

ὀρέγω (L.S.) 'reach' is considered a case of prothesis by Lejeune and Schwyzer, but because of the quality of the initial vowel, a compound of ὀ- (as in ὀκέλλω), and the root *reg- seen in Lat. *regō* by Frisk (2.413). Szemerényi (1964:227) accounts for the ὀ- as an analogical form of *ἀρεγ- or *ἐρεγ- after the *ā*-stem noun *ἀρογā or *ἐρογā assimilated to *ὀρογā. Since he connects the word with IE *reg-, he can thus assume prothesis. Schwyzer also cites in this connection the form ὀρόγυια (Pi. *P.* 4.228, Ar. *Fr.* 942), a longer form of ὄργυια 'length of the outstretched arms' which is in turn a syncopated form of *ὠρόγυια (Szemerényi 1964:231) or ὀρόγυια (Frisk 2.412). Though this word has problems of its own, it seems clear enough that the *o*-color of the initial vowel can have arisen because of the influence of the following -/u/-: *arguia > *orguia. This ὄργυια in turn, however it arose, can have caused the initial vowel in the whole family of words to become ὀ-. The *ar- in *arguia can either be original, or (and this is more likely [cf. Skt. r̥júḥ 'straight']) stem from *[r̥].

All of these examples, if we omit ἐρυθρός and ὄροφος as analogical, have an /e/-vowel after the /r/-, and in all certain cases the /e/-vowel is short: ἀρήγω really cannot be counted a sure instance of prothesis. The /e/ is then in turn followed either by -RC-, or by a voiced sound (Ἔρεβος, ὀρέγω) or by an aspirate (ἐρέφω). On the basis of this distributional information we might be tempted to write a rule:

$$/r/ > /ər/ \ /\_e \begin{bmatrix} \text{Voiced Consonant} \\ \text{Aspirate} \end{bmatrix}$$

Or, since we still want a devoicing rule:

$$/r/ > /hr/ \ /\_e[\text{Voiceless, Non-aspirated}]$$

$$/ər/ \ /\_e \text{ elsewhere}$$

Thus all */r/- become aspirated before /e/ followed by a voiceless non-aspirated consonant, and all remaining */re/- (and presumably */ri/-, had there been any) pass then to *əre-. About */r/- before other vowels we will see in a moment.

6.2.2 With this distributional information acquired, we can examine other possible cases of prothesis. Schwyzer includes ἐρέπτομαι 'feed on', a rare epic verb used only of granivorous animals (LSJ) in the present participle, compounded *ἀνερέπομαι (generally recorded as ἀνερειπ-). This word is usually connected (Frisk 1.553) with Lith. ap-rĕpti 'fassen, ergreifen', and less immediately with Lat. rapiō 'snatch'. This example has the proper vowel, but the voiceless sound (if not from -pʰ-) goes against the definition just given.

Schwyzer also includes ὀρύσσω 'dig', together with all its compounds. Frisk (2.430-431), also feeling that the ὀ- is prothetic, compares Lat. runcō 'weed' and Lett. rūkēt 'wühlen, scharren', neither one a particularly convincing etymology, especially since the Grk. aspirate in these words is then isolated. Frisk also proposes as a possibility connection with οὑρός 'trench, channel', on the assumption that the guttural is suffixal. Again, and in either event, the ὀ- may be rounded from ἀ- by the following -/u/-, so that the original root may well have been *aru-. If such should be the original form of the root, it opens up the possibilty at least of connection with ἄρουρα 'tilled land', generally derived from *arowr̥ (Frisk 1.147, Chantraine 1968:113) and Lat. aruus 'plowed, arable' (Walde-Hofmann 1.71). Prothesis is then excluded.

ἐρωή 'quick motion, rush, force' (Il. 3.62) and ἐρωέω 'rush forth' (Il. 1.303) is also included by Schwyzer. These words cannot be accommodated by the rule suggested above, and if the usual etymological connections with Germanic words derived from PIE *rōsā is maintained, then that rule cannot stand. But beside these forms there exists on the one hand the verb ῥώομαι 'move with speed or violence' and the homophones ἐρωή 'rest from' and ἐρωέω 'draw back or rest from' which, taken together, indicate that two (largely epic) nouns and their verbal derivates have become confused. This of course does not explicate the prothesis in one or the other of these words, but as Frisk says, the whole group of words requires reinvestigation. If ἐρωέω is in fact, as he suggests, an intensive deverbative, the base of these words may have been *res-, which would in fact have developed to *reh- > *əreh-. *rōh-, however, did not develop prothesis since -/o:/- does not allow prothesis (6.2.4).

6.2.3 Thus none of Schwyzer's examples provides a real obstacle to the rule, though perhaps my judgment has been colored by my desire to create a rule. Other potential cases of prothesis may be mentioned here. ἐρέχθω 'rend, break' (Il. 23.317) fits the rule, and is usually connected with Skt. rakṣas- 'Zerstörung, Beschädigung' (Frisk 1.557). ἐρῳδιός (Il. 10.274) 'heron' with its by-forms ῥῳδιός (Hippon. 63) and ἀρῳδιός (v.l. LXX Le. 11.19, al.) could belong, but its history is too unclear for any definite conclusion (cf. Frisk 1.572-573). ὀροθύνω (Il. 10.332) 'stir up, arouse' might be included, but is an epic word only, and is considered by Frisk (2.424) a secondary formation to ἐρέθω. It must in some way be connected also with ὄρνυμι, and hence is not a case of prothesis.

6.2.4 The rule can therefore be stated: */r/- > */ər/- only before /e/ followed by a voiced or aspirated consonant. But we have as yet said nothing about initial */ra/- */ro/- */ru/-, or, indeed, about */sr/- and */wr/-. Since prothesis does not develop before them, we will have to write the rules in such a way that they fall through the rules without developing prothesis, but do become aspirated. This can be done in a number of ways, unfortunately. For the moment the simplest way is to assume that:

$$\begin{bmatrix} sr \\ wr \end{bmatrix}\text{-} \quad > \quad \text{/hr/-}$$

$$\text{/r/-} \quad > \quad \text{/ər/\_\_e}\begin{bmatrix} \text{Voiced Consonant} \\ \text{Aspirated Consonant} \end{bmatrix}$$

$$> \quad \text{/hr/ elsewhere}$$

Clearly this scheme is oversimplified, and puts too much into a single set of rules, but it will do for the moment: we will reintroduce complexity, and I hope versimilitude, when we integrate /r/- with the other semivowels.

6.3.0 With */w/- things are more difficult, for there are three developments, not two: in addition to developing prothesis before $\begin{bmatrix} e \\ i \end{bmatrix}$RC, /w/ appears normally as Ø in later dialects (cf. ἔτος 'year'), but also as /h/ (cf. ἴστωρ 'judge'). Sommer (1905: 119-122) considered this latter development the exception, and attributed the aspiration to syllable-final -/s/- or -/r/- before a voiceless consonant. His rule has, however, not fared well because of the word ἄστυ 'town' which is not accounted for by it. But if we adopt and adapt part of the formulation given above for */r/-, this word is no longer an exception, for it will be unaffected by a rule:

$$\text{*/w/-} > \text{*/hw/- /\_\_}\begin{bmatrix} e \\ i \end{bmatrix}\text{Voiceless Consonant}$$

All we need do is assume that, though */r/- > */hr/- before

THE REASONS   101

non-front vowels, */w/- did not: this rule will account for the
aspiration in:

ἑκών   'readily'   < *wekōn   (Frisk 1.479)
ἕννυμι   'put clothes on'   (Frisk 1.521-522)
            with aspiration after ἕσσα (5.3.5)
ἕσπερος   'at evening'   < *wesperos   (Frisk 1.575)
ἑστία   'hearth'   < *westiā   (Frisk 1.576-577)
ἵστωρ   'judge'   < *wistōr   (Frisk 1.740-741)

But it fails to account for the lack of aspiration in a number of
words like ἔτος and ἔπος which should have aspiration.[50]

6.3.1 A fact not mentioned by Sommer in his discussion of
aspiration in words deriving from *wes- (1905:115) is that not all
words containing *wes- are aspirated. For, though ἕννυμι and εἷμα
and ἱμάτιον are aspirated, ἔσθος and ἐσθής are not. Since we have
no particular reason to believe that these words were not present
in PGrk., we must assume that there occurred a dissimilation of
aspiration which caused *hwesthos and *hwesthēs to develop to
*westhos and *westhēs. Hence Sommer's rule, as reformulated in
the last paragraph, must be followed by another rule which
dissimilates aspiration, a rule which will also cause dissimilation
of aspiration in words with initial */hw/- < */sw/-, at least
before /e/ and /i/. Hence the following become regular:

ἔαρ   'spring'   < *wehar < *hwehar
                                       (Frisk 1.432-433)
ἔθνος   'band'   < *swedh-   (Frisk 1.448-449)
ἔθος   'custom'   < *swedh-   (Frisk 1.449)
ἔθων   'be accustomed' < *wedh-   (Frisk 1.449-450)

---

[50] There are, to be sure, late instances of ἔτος, and one might be inclined
to assume that this form, since it conforms to the rule, is legitimate and old.
And indeed we will see in 6.3.1 that a paradigm *hwetos *wetehos must at one
time have existed. But I am dissuaded, reluctantly, from making this
assumption both by the late date of the examples and by the fact that
aspiration occurs also in other words (ἴδιος ἐφεῖδε) from which the rule
excludes aspiration, as well as in ἴσος, for which aspiration might well be
predicted. Rather, all must have received the aspiration secondarily by analogy
with other words (Sommer 1905: 105-107).

ἔορ   'sister'   < *hwehor   (Frisk 1.530-531)
ἐσθής ἐσθός
ἔχω   'bring'   < *weghō   (Frisk 1.604)
ἰσχύς   'strength'   < *wisghus   (Frisk 1.742-743,
                                              above 5.8.6)

Several cases, however, are not even yet picked up, but they will be, if we do not demand that the aspiration appear in the immediately succeeding consonant (cluster). If we accept this condition, we find that we can include the remaining exceptions:[51]

ἔπος   'word' after *wekʷehos   < *hwekʷehos (Frisk 1.545)
ἔτος   'year' after *wetehos   < *hwetehos (Frisk 1.583-584)

6.3.2 It seems that the following formulation, again later to be integrated with other initial semivowels, will handle developments involving */w/-:

$$/sw/- \quad > \quad -/hw/-$$

$$/w/- \quad > \quad /\mathring{w}/- \ / \_\_\begin{bmatrix} e \\ i \end{bmatrix} \text{Voiceless}$$

---

[51] Notice that this rule will account also for the lack of aspiration in ἀδελφός 'brother' (Frisk 1.19, Chantraine 1968:19) and ἄλοχος 'wife' (Frisk 1.1, Chantraine 1968:2), as has been correctly pointed out by Solmsen (1901:223) and Chantraine (1968:2). The aspiration rule will account also for the following cases not usually considered to contain initial */w/- if we should wish to include them: ἔκηλος 'at one's ease' (Frisk 1.477), ἔξ 'six' (Frisk 1.527-528), ἔκαστος 'each' (Frisk 1.473), ἔρκος (Frisk 1.561 and 6.3.3 below), ἔταιρος (Frisk 1.579). But there are exceptions even at that: ἔταλον 'yearling' < *wetalon (Frisk 1.579) occurs only twice in all of Grk. (Schwyzer 1923: 644.18, 252.11), both times in inscriptions of the third century, and both times from psilotic dialect areas. Hence the word may originally have had */h/-. But if it did not, we can certainly invoke the analogy of ἔτος. ἐανός 'fine robe' < *wesanos (Frisk 1.432) should have no /h/-, but has received it by analogy with ἔννυμι. ἴσκω 'make like' is a shortened form of ἐΐσκω (5.8.4). ἴσος 'equal' (Frisk 1.737-738) is problematic, and I really cannot account for the psilosis. But ἴσος does occur (Schwyzer 1923:708a 1), and Homeric ἶσος and ἐΐση (with prothesis — 2.4.6) make this word's history particularly problematic. ἔτης 'clansman' (Frisk 1.581-582) derives from */sw/-, so definitely should show */h/- because there is no other aspirate in the word to cause it to disappear. I cannot explain the psilosis in this word or in ἴτυς 'felloe' (Frisk 1.743-744).

/w̥/-   >   /hw/-

/hw/-   >   /w/ /__Aspiration

$$/\text{w}/\text{-} \quad > \quad /\text{əw}/\text{-}\underline{\quad}\begin{bmatrix}\begin{bmatrix}e\\i\end{bmatrix}RC \\ Aspiration\begin{bmatrix}r\\l\end{bmatrix}\end{bmatrix}$$

> /w/ elsewhere

6.3.3 Voiceless sounds include not only voiceless stops and /s/. Sommer (1905:127-130) had the further merit of explaining the various forms of ἔργω (εἴργω εἵργω, ἔρξα ἔρξα) as the result of a blend of *ewerg- with prothesis and *herks- with aspiration developing before */w/ followed by voiceless /r/: the /r/ is voiceless by reason of the following voiceless consonant. (For the relevant forms cf. Solmsen 1901: 221-224.) We have repeatedly seen above (particularly 5.9.0) that prothetic forms alternate with non-prothetic forms only in syllables closed with /r/ (ἔεδνον ~ ἔδνον (2.4.1) is not relevant — cf. n. 33). Examples are ὀμόργνυμι ~ μόρξαντο (2.2.6), ἔνεροι, νέρτεροι ~ ἐνέρτεροι, νέρθεν ~ ἔνερθεν (2.3.3), ἐέργω ~ ἔρξας (2.4.3), ἐέρση ~ ἔρση (2.4.5), ἀμέρδω ~ μέρδει (3.2.7). Sommer's rule is most likely to be correct, and if we accept it and give it a certain extension, we can then account also for the lack of prothesis in some at least of the above forms by assuming an alternation between syllables closed by voiced [r] (appearing before voiced or aspirated consonants or /s/) and voiceless [r̥] (appearing before voiceless consonants). On this assumption ὀμόργνυμι and ἐέργω are obviously regular, though μόρξαντο is more likely to be analogical, as we have seen; ἀμέρδω is regular if we assume that μέρδει comes from the aorist *μέρσαι; ἔνερθεν is regular, as is νέρτερος, and νέρθεν and ἐνέρτερος ἔνεροι must be analogical; and even ἐέρση ~ ἔρση can be accounted for if we assume that ἐέρση is the regular continuation of *wersā and hence directly comparable with Skt. varṣa-, while ἔρση comes from a *wertsa remodeled after ἄρδω < *werdo (cf. Eustath. 1625: ἀπὸ τοῦ ἄρδω, ἄρσω ἢ ἔρση γίνεται). On this assumption the other forms become yet clearer, and we get another clue as to the phonological stage of the Grk. language at which prothesis developed: -/ts/- had not yet developed to -/s/-, but contrasted with it, at least after /r/: /r/ was voiced before /s/: ἐέρση, but was voiceless before /t(s)/ and /k(s)/: μόρξαντο (?) νέρτεροι ἔρξας *wertsai *mertsai.[52]

6.4.0 A word or two about /u/ seems necessary. The ordinary view, which must be essentially correct, would seem to hold that all PIE */u/- develop to */hu/- in Grk. But we have seen above (4.1.3, 4.4.2, n. 38) that there are cases in which */u/- has been thought to develop to */əu/ (> */eu/- or */au/-), and indeed that Wackernagel (1953: 654-655) held that all initial */u/- in Grk. developed to */au/-. The only cases in which we have been tempted to admit this development are that of */uh/- > */auh/- in ἰαύω (4.4.2 above), and that can be handled by assuming that */u/- > */hu/- save before */h/-; and ἀλώπηξ (4.1.3). But there are a number of other cases in which */u/- is thought to have passed to */əu/- before */l/ and */r/, and it might be well to go through them here.[53]

---

[52] Just as /r/ was voiceless before a voiceless consonant, so it is possible that /l/ was also under certain conditions. If we assume that /l/ was voiceless before /i/, or at least induced voicelessness in initial */w/- which then passed to */hw/-, we can explain the aspiration in ἑλίκη 'willow' (Frisk 1.494) and ἕλιξ 'spiral' together with its derivatives (Frisk 1.495-496), all from *weli-. And just as the /r/ induced aspiration in initial resonants even after /a/ (cf. *marks-, etc. 2.2.6, 6.3.3), so may /li/. If so, we can then account for the aspiration in ἁλίσκομαι if from *wali (Frisk 1.74, Chantraine 1968:62; aspiration secondary after αἱρέω — Sommer 1905:101-102), and ἅλις 'in heaps', if from earlier *walis (Frisk 1.74, Chantraine 1968:62) and not from *swalis (Sommer 1905:112).

[53] There are two words in which a prothetic vowel is thought to have developed before /u/- not followed by /r/ or /l/. But εὔκηλος 'free from care' beside ἕκηλος < *wekalos does not derive from a weak-grade form *ukalos, but is merely a "volksetymologische Umbildung nach den vielen Komposita mit εὐ-" (Frisk 1.477). αὐδή 'human voice' is more difficult because it seems clearly cognate with Skt. vádati 'speak', part. uditá. The only way to make this connection is to assume that an original *ud- in Skt. was included in regular verbal categories by means of the insertion of /e/ (> *wed-) but developed prothesis (> *əud-) in Grk. But if we do assume *ud- > *əud-,

6.4.1 Cases of prothesis developing before */ur/- are neither very numerous nor very convincing.

εὑρίσκω 'find' has been thought to come from earlier *ἐ-ϝρεῖν with prothetic ἐ- (Frisk 1.591-592), but this is highly unlikely, and leaves the aspiration unexplained. Furthermore, from *ewr- one might expect *eir-, cf. εἴρηκα < *(w)ewr-. *ur- > *ǝur- might be a possibility, though other IE forms do point rather to *wre-.

Εὐρύλαος and other Εὐρυ- names beside Ἐρύλαος, etc., can be explained in three ways: analogy of εὐρύς, metathesis (*weru- > euru-), and prothesis (*uru- > euru-: Frisk 1.569). Probably analogy is the proper explanation, but *ur- > *ǝur- > eur- seems not impossible. If we adopt this explanation, however, we will then have to assume that *euru- > *eru- with dissimilation of the first */u/ in all *eru- forms of the verb (ἔρυμαι, ἐρύομαι 'protect, guard'), and we will be unable to account for those forms with initial ῥ- (ῥυσίπολις, etc.) An alternation *weru- ~ *wru- seems most likely for this verb, and hence no prothesis in personal names containing *euru-. My own feeling is that Εὐρύλαος, etc., is a deformation after εὐρύς of the no longer understood *Εἰρύλαος which contains the longer stem form εἰρ- (< *wewr- n. 55 below) of the verb *weru-.

εὐρύς 'broad, wide' is definitely connected with Skt. urú- (Frisk 1.593), and hence is perhaps as likely a candidate as there is for prothesis in Grk. But Indo-Iranian initial unaccented */au/- of whatever origin always develops to */u/- (Wyatt

---

then we are in the uncomfortable position of being unable to explain ὑδέω 'call, name' (Call. Fr. anon. 62) and ὕδη = φήμη ᾠδή, both of which show regular aspiration; and even if we discard these forms as being attested only late, we are still embarrassed by ὕδωρ ὕδατος which should show *ǝu- as well. Rather, distasteful as it may seem, I feel we should give up direct connection of αὐδή and vadati and connect αὐδή rather with αὔω 'shout out' (Frisk 1.193, Chantraine 1968:145), either directly, i.e. < *au- or on the assumption that *ud- > *aud- on the analogy of αὔω. Solmsen (1901:266-267) felt that αὐδή had ἀ- of analogical origin because prothesis developed only before semivocalic u̯, not before the vowel u. I have assumed that prothesis develops before */ul/- and */ur/- rather than before */wl/- and */wr/- because as we shall see (6.4.4), and indeed as is well known, */wl/- and */wr/- pass to */l/- and */r/- respectively.

1970:26-28), so the chances are equally good that the IE form was
*eurús, and not *urús (so Beekes 1969:287). Since two rules are
potentially operative in this case, and since both give the correct
results, it is impossible to decide on phonological grounds what
the original IE form was, though *urús seems more likely on
morphophonemic grounds; for though it is not the case that lack
of IE accent necessarily implies reduced grade, it is the case
that presence of accent does imply full (e/o) grade (cf. Wyatt
1970:56-59).

εὐρώς 'mould' has been connected by Solmsen (1901:123 n. 1)
with Skt. vṛṇoti 'cover' on the assumption of an earlier *ἐ-ϝρώς
with prothetic vowel. But the etymology is in fact unknown
(Frisk 1.594), and my rules would predict *εἰρώς from *ewrōs.
Nonetheless if we assume with Schwyzer (1939:514) an original
-s- stem, then it may be possible to keep Solmsen's etymology if
we can assume that the genitive (and oblique cases generally) of
this word experienced the following development: *wrosos >
*hwrosos > *hwrohos > *wrohos = *urohos > *eurohos (or
perhaps better: *wrosos > *wrohos = *urohos > *eurohos) with
the regular aspiration of */wr/- dissimilated by the following
-/h/- (cf. below 6.4.3).

6.4.2 Instances of a similar development before */ul/- are more
secure, even though the details in many cases are unclear.

ἄλοξ 'furrow' beside αὖλαξ, ὦλαξ, εὐλάκα 'plough-share' (forms
assembled at Frisk 1.77) are all related, and must somehow derive
from a single form. We have supposed above (n. 40) that that
form was *auloks, and that it lost the */u/ by dissimilation on
the one hand; on the other the */o/ of the second syllable must
have passed to /a/. There is no reason thus far to assume
prothesis, but the */au/ ∼ */eu/ alternation and the generally
accepted etymology do lead us in that direction. We may
therefore assume an original *ulok-.

εὐλή 'worm' is a less certain instance since ἐ-ϝλή and further
etymological connection with εἰλέω, etc. (Frisk 1.588) is uncertain. But if we accept the connection, then we must suppose that
*ula : *wlā would yield *λή.

εὔληρα 'reins', Doric αὔληρα may be connected with the root
εἰλέω , and if so requires prothesis, a development apparently
vouched for also by the different vowel qualities within Grk.
Schwyzer (1939:224) and Frisk (1.588) assume *ἐ-ϝληρ-ο, *ἀ-
ϝληρ-ο and connection with Lat. *lōrum* < *wlōr-*. We must, if
this plausible connection is to be kept, assume that original *ulōr-*
passed to *wlōr-* in Lat. and thence to *lōr-*, but that its sister
ulēr- developed prothesis in Grk.

6.4.3 Though few of these cases by themselves seem certain, taken
as a group they do indeed point to a rule $*u\begin{bmatrix}r\\l\end{bmatrix}$- > $*\mathrm{ə}u\begin{bmatrix}r\\l\end{bmatrix}$-. There
are only a few examples which might tend to cast doubt on this
rule, but: ὑλάν 'bark' and its derivatives are clearly onomatopoetic; ὕλη 'forest' may come from *seu-* (Frisk 2.962-963) if
indeed the etymology is known; ὕλλος 'a fish' < *udlos* (Frisk
2.963); ὕρχη 'jar' is probably a Phoenician loan (Frisk 2.973).
Hence none of these examples serves to contravene a rule:[54]

$$*/u/- \; > \quad /u/\, /\_\_\begin{bmatrix}r\\l\end{bmatrix}$$
$$> \quad /hu/ \text{ elsewhere}$$
$$*/u/ \; > \quad /\mathrm{ə}u/$$

6.4.4 When we ask ourselves the reason for this at first sight
strange development, we find that it is really quite comprehen-

---

[54] One wonders whether the rule ought not to be extended to include
*/um/- and */un/- as well. Wackernagel (1953:654) compared Grk. εὖνις
'bereaved of' with Skt. *ūná-* 'unzureichend, ermangelnd' on the assumption
that the Grk. form shows prothesis (Frisk 1.589). And εὐνή 'bed', if connected
with Ave. *unā* 'Lock, Riss (in der Erde)' (Frisk *ibid.*) might show the same
development. And perhaps ἐμέω 'vomit' finds its explanation in this way.
Nowhere in Grk. is there any trace of the initial */w/- demanded for this
word by its cognates Lat. *vomo* and Skt. *vámiti*, and its compounds generally
show the lengthening normal in words with initial vowel (Frisk 1.504-505). I
am not sure that the following is any improvement, but if we can assume a
basic *umé-* or even *um-*, we might be tempted to suppose the development:
umé > *əumé* > *eumé* (with prothetic vowel) > *emé* (by some sort of
dissimilatory loss of labiality before the following /m/). Hence we get ἐμέω,
but the price may seem too great.

sible, for only before /r l/ could /w/ also appear, as for instance in:

ῥήτωρ	'orator'	<	*wrḗtōr	(Frisk 1.470)
ῥίζα	'root'	<	*wridya	(Frisk 2.655-656)
ῥινός	'skin'	<	*wrīnos	(Frisk 2.657-658)
ῥόδον	'rose'	<	*wrodon	(Frisk 2.660-661)
λάσιος	'hairy'	<	*wlatios	(Frisk 2.88)
λύκος	'wolf'	<	*wlkʷos	(Frisk 2.143-144)
λῆνος	'wool'	<	*wlīnos	(Frisk 2.117)

And as [w] > [hw] before /r l/, so the distinctively voiced */u/ > */əu/ in the same environment.[55]

[55] Numerous words have been assumed to contain initial */wr/-, but sometimes on insufficient grounds. All those etymologies, for instance, which are based on the occurrence of βρ- in Aeolic poets are suspect, for when one looks through the poems and fragments in *PLF* one discovers only a few cases of ρ-, and that of these none is metrically secure, while many cases of βρ- are. Hence it is very likely the case that in psilotic Lesbian */hr/- and */wr/- merged, but in */wr/-, not in */hr/ as elsewhere. Hence the fact that Sappho has βραδίναν (102.2) is not evidence that the word once began with */w/-. It is furthermore likely that cases of βρ- quoted by grammarians, such as Βραδάμανθος, are in fact drawn from Aeolic poets and are also not to be used as evidence for earlier */wr/-. And this brings us in turn to a further point about the early Greek treatments of */wr/- and */sr/-. They behave exactly alike initially (ἔρρεεν, ἔρρεξα) and this fact, taken together with the Lesbian developments just mentioned, would suggest that they merged completely in initial position, perhaps in [hwr]-. If they merged initially, we might well expect them to have merged internally as well, again probably as [hwr]-. That they did in fact so merge seems proved by examples of perfects with compensatory lengthening like (Lejeune 1955:154) εἴρημαι < *wewrēmai, εἴρυμαι < *wewrūmai; εἴλυμαι < *wewlūmai (cf. εἴληφα < *seslāpʰa, εἵμαρται < *sesmrtai, ἴληθι < *sislātʰi). Again there is a parallel development which suggests that *wewr- > *wehwr- > *wehr- > *wēr, rather than that *wewr- passed to *weir- by dissimilation, the usual explanation. It is not necessary, or even indicated, to assume that *sl- > *hwl- > *hl, though it is of course necessary to assume *wl- > *hwl- > *hl-. But there are a number of cases in which *wr > ur (Lejeune *ibid.*): ταλαύρινος 'bearing a shield of bull's hide' (*Il.* 5.289) < *ταλα-ϝρινος (Frisk 2.657-658); καλαῦροψ 'shepherd's staff' (*Il.* 23.845) < *καλα-ϝροψ (Frisk 1.762); ἀπούρας 'take

6.5.0 Developments involving initial */y/- (Wyatt 1969a) also belong here, and must be fitted into the scheme of aspiration-prothesis, even though prothesis does not develop before */y/-. When we consider the examples, we find that the same rules, though of different extent of application, are required as for */w/-, namely /y/ > /hy/ and /hy/ > /y/: a further pair of rules, /hy/ > /h/ and /y/ > /dy/ completes the series.

6.5.1 There are only a few cases of initial */y/-, and it might be well to list them here:

| ἥβα | 'youth' | < *yḗgʷā | (Frisk 1.620) |
| ἧπαρ | 'liver' | < *yḗkʷṛt | (Frisk 1.639) |

---

away' (*Il.* 1.356) < *ἀπο-ϝρας (Frisk 1.125), αὔρηκτος 'unbroken' (Hdn. 2.171) < ἀ-ϝρηκτος (Frisk 2.652-653). These all show /w/ > /u/ counter to the rule just established whereby /w/ > [hw] > /h/. But it is to be noticed that in all cases the preceding vowel was /a/ or /o/, whereas it was /e/ in all previous cases. This fact suggests the rule:

$$w\begin{bmatrix} r \\ l \end{bmatrix} \ > \ hw\begin{bmatrix} r \\ l \end{bmatrix} \ > \ /h/\begin{bmatrix} e \\ i \end{bmatrix}\_$$

$$> \ /w/\begin{bmatrix} a \\ o \end{bmatrix}\_$$

a rule which looks very much like the rule (Lejeune 1955:134) affecting $\begin{bmatrix} r \\ n \end{bmatrix}$y-, and which is most likely merely a part of it, a fact possibly borne out by the words πολύρην (= [polūrēn]), which may be the correct interpretation of πολύρρην 'rich in lambs' (*Il.* 9.154, Frisk 1.137-138) and πολύριζος for πολύρριζος 'with many roots' (Thphr. *HP* 9.10.2). But if the rule can be so set up, then there is nothing preventing us from assuming that *sr- is to be included as well:

$$\begin{bmatrix} s \\ w \end{bmatrix}r \ > \ [hwr]$$
$$[hwr] > [hr]/\begin{bmatrix} e \\ i \\ u \end{bmatrix}\_$$
$$[ur]/\begin{bmatrix} a \\ o \end{bmatrix}\_$$

If the rule is to be formulated in this way, then we cannot use the occurrence of -ur- as evidence for earlier *wr-. In general this fact will make little difference, except that now we can connect Grk. ῥήγνυμι 'break' with Lat. *frango* 'break', if we should want to, on the assumption of original *sr-.

εἰνατέρες	'sisters-in-law'	< *yenateres	(Frisk 1.464)
			with psilosis
ὅς	'who' (rel.)	< *yos	(Frisk 2.434)
ὥρα	'season'	< *yōr-	(Frisk 2.1151)
ὑσμίνα	'battle'	< *yudh-	(Frisk 2.974)
ζειαί	'spelt'	< *yewya (?)	(Frisk 1.608-609)
ζέω	'boil'	< *yes-	(Frisk 1.612)
ζωστός	'girded'	< *yōs-	(Frisk 1.617-618)
ζυγόν	'yoke'	< *yugom	(Frisk 1.615-616)
ζύμη	'leaven'	< *yūs-	(Frisk 1.616)

From this list we see that */y/- > */hy/- before /e o/ and before /us/ or /uts/ (< *yudhs-), but remains elsewhere (in *yug-; and *yūh- < *yūs- by the rule /s/ > /h/). This situation is to be taken as rule 1), a rule which aspirates initial */y/- in most environments. A second rule, a dissimilation of aspiration rule, will cause /hy/ to pass to /y/ (or prevent /y/ from developing to /hy/). Hence 'boil' passes through two stages: *hyehō by rule one, *yehō by rule two, and similarly with 'gird' (*hyōhnūmi > *yōhnūmi) and 'spelt' (hyehwya > *yehwya). Subsequent rules cause */y/- to develop to */dy/- and */hy/- to develop to */h/-. And since the failure of */yu/- to pass to *[hyu]- seems explicable only in terms of the previous passage of */u/- to *[hyu]-, we can list the rules in the following order (which differs slightly from that given in Wyatt 1969a):

1)   /u/   >   [hyu]/__[non-liquid]

2)   /y/   >   [hy]/__$\begin{bmatrix} \text{mid-vowel} \\ \text{/us/} \end{bmatrix}$

3)   /s/   >   /h/

4)   [hy]   >   /y/ /__[Vh]

5)   [hy]   >   /h/

6)   /y/   >   /dy/

These rules produce the correct results.[56]

[56] Since all initial */u/- in Grk. pass to */hu/-, we might expect that all */i/- would as well. But here we are troubled by the facts that there are very

6.6.0 It is now time to draw together all the rules presented above and to put them into a coherent whole. It is clear that, though there is considerable diversity in detail, certain main tendencies do stand out. They are:

1) the devoicing of initial resonants

2) the passage of /s/ > /h/

3) the merger of [R̥] and [hR] in /hR/

4) dissimilation of the aspiration arising in proto-Greek times from the above developments: this type of dissimilation is to be kept quite separate from that of IE date whereby $*t^hit^h\bar{e}mi$ $(*d^hid^h\bar{e}mi) > *tit^h\bar{e}mi$.

5) development of a prothetic vowel in the relevant environments

6) remaining developments involving resonants not affected by rules 1) or 5). As the reader will already have seen, problems arise only in connection with rules 1) and 5) and the extent of their application. Perhaps it will be most convenient to take up the main tendencies one at a time.

6.6.1 The rules presented in earlier sections which have to do with the devoicing of initial resonants include (in some cases rephrased):

$$6.1.2 \ [R] > [R̥] \text{ save in } \begin{bmatrix} e \\ a \\ i \end{bmatrix} RC$$

$$6.2.4 \ /r/ > [hr]/\_\_ \begin{bmatrix} \begin{bmatrix} e \\ i \end{bmatrix} \text{voiceless} \\ \text{non-front vowels /a o u/} \end{bmatrix}$$

$$6.3.2 \ /w/ > [hw]/\_\_ \begin{bmatrix} \begin{bmatrix} e \\ i \end{bmatrix} \text{voiceless} \\ \begin{bmatrix} r \\ l \end{bmatrix} \text{vowel} \end{bmatrix}$$

few cases of initial */i/- for which we can establish a good etymology and that many */i/- occur as a syllable of reduplication and can be suspected of containing the aspiration of the unreduplicated form. In order to settle this question definitively an entire separate investigation would be necessary. But for the moment at least, and with all due caution, it is to be noted than an aspiration rule will account for the unexplained aspiration in ἵππος (Frisk 1.733-735).

6.4.3 /u/ > [u]/__$\begin{bmatrix} r \\ l \end{bmatrix}$

[hu] / elsewhere

6.5.1 /y/ > [hy]/__$\begin{bmatrix} a\ e\ o \\ u/\_s \end{bmatrix}$

There are many things common to all these rules, which is not surprising, and we can see that front vowels and voiceless consonants seem to play a large role. We may then reformulate the devoicing rule (omitting /a/) as follows:

a)   [R]   >   [R̥]/__$\begin{bmatrix} e \\ i \end{bmatrix}$voiceless

This formulation will handle almost all of 6.1.2, one half of 6.2.4 in its newer form without non-aspirate specified, one half of 6.3.2, and a small part of 6.5.1. The remainder of 6.1.2 can be included if we add:

a1) $\begin{bmatrix} l \\ m \end{bmatrix}$ >   [R̥]/__/a/ Voiceless

This rule will allow ἀμαλδύνω (2.2.5) *ἀμάργνυμι (2.2.6) ἐλαφρός (2.1.4) ἐλάσσων (2.1.5) to be affected by rule 5) by providing a contrast between [l m] and [l̥ m̥] before /a/ as well as before front vowels. If we should wish for any reason (5.8.0) to exclude /a/ from the class of vowels before which prothesis can occur, or if we do not feel that a contrast between [l] and [l̥] is necessary in order for prothesis to develop before /l/, we can do without this modification and stick with a). Again, in order to accomodate the irregular Homeric scansion of short vowels as constituting a heavy syllable before λόφος, etc. (=[llopʰos]), we could have a rule which devoices all the true resonants (/l m n r/) before back vowels (or perhaps only rounded vowels). This rule will incorporate the remainder of 6.1.2 and 6.2.4 and will appear as:

a2) /l m n r/ >   [R̥]/__/a o u/

If we do not, we will need a different a2) to handle /r/:

a2′) /r/   >   [R̥]/__/a o u/

We will in our final formulation adopt both these rules, though allowing aspiration before /a/ only to /r/ since doing so will account for many data and is not falsified by any. We will therefore write:

$$/l\ m\ n\ r/\ >\ [\mathring{R}]/\_\_\text{rounded vowels}$$

$$/r/\ >\ [\mathring{r}]/\_\_/a/$$

The rule presented in 6.4.3 should probably appear at the head of the list because its output is required for 6.5.1, but putting it here will cause no difficulty. It should be rephrased in its second part, and the second half of 6.3.2 added as a4):

a3) /u/   > $/u/\ /\_\_\begin{bmatrix} r \\ l \end{bmatrix}$

[ẙu]/ elsewhere

a4) /w/   > $[\mathring{R}]/\_\_\begin{bmatrix} r \\ l \end{bmatrix}\text{Vowel}$

Then 6.5.1 can be inserted as is, and the whole series of sections of rule 1) will be:

1 - a)   [R]   > $[\mathring{R}]/\_\_\begin{bmatrix} e \\ i \end{bmatrix}\text{voiceless}$

b)   /l m n r/ > $[\mathring{R}]/\_\_/a\ o\ u/\ ([\mathring{r}]=[\mathring{w}\mathring{r}])$

c)   /u/   > $/u/\ /\_\_\begin{bmatrix} r \\ l \end{bmatrix}\text{vowel}$

[ů]/__elsewhere ([ů]=[ẙu])

d)   /w/   > $[\mathring{R}]/\_\_\begin{bmatrix} r \\ l \end{bmatrix}\text{vowel}$

e)   /y/   > $[\mathring{R}]/\_\_\begin{bmatrix} e\ a\ o \\ u/\_\_s \end{bmatrix}$

6.6.2 The first rule, not only because it initiates the whole chain of events which culminates in prothesis, but also because of the great variety of developments affecting the individual sounds, has been the most difficult to formulate and is, accordingly, the most likely to prove incorrect in detail: it must be correct in its main outlines. Rules 2) and 3) are everywhere the same, and the only real question is whether they should be kept as two separate rules or be rephrased as only one. I prefer to keep them separate, and formulate them as follows (for the environments relevant to this work):

2) /s/ > /h/ / $\begin{bmatrix} V \\ R \\ \# \end{bmatrix}$ __ $\begin{bmatrix} V \\ R \end{bmatrix}$

3) [R̊] > [hR]

6.6.3 The fourth rule as formulated first in 6.1.2 called for [hR] to pass to [R] before aspiration only when that aspiration was in turn followed by [R]. But that formulation turned out to be too narrow, would have required more dissimilation rules later on, and hence was broadened to the rule which appears at the end of 6.1.2, a rule which can remain as is with only the specification of the following vowel added:

4) [hR] > [R]/__ $\begin{bmatrix} a \\ e \\ i \end{bmatrix}$ Aspirate

i.e., before non-rounded vowels. This rule picks up one half of the aspiration rule involving /r/ given in 6.2.4 and left by the side in 6.6.1, and provides that henceforth /l m n r y w/ will appear voiced (unaspirated) before unrounded vowels in a syllable closed by [R] and before aspiration.

6.6.4 Rule 5) is of course the rule which occasioned the establishment of the preceding rules, and will be seen also to provide the residue which feeds into rule 6). The formulation given in 6.1.2 can stand as is, but perhaps at this point had best be separated into two parts in order to reflect the discussion of 6.6.1 above concerning resonants before /a/:

5) [R] > [əR]/__ $\begin{bmatrix} e \\ i \end{bmatrix} \begin{bmatrix} RC \\ Asp \begin{bmatrix} l \\ r \end{bmatrix} \end{bmatrix}$

$$[\text{lm}] \quad > \quad [\text{əR}]/\_\_/a/ \begin{bmatrix} \begin{bmatrix} l \\ r \end{bmatrix}C \\ \text{Asp}\begin{bmatrix} r \\ y \end{bmatrix} \end{bmatrix}$$

The second half of this rule allows us to include the exceptions mentioned in 6.6.1. Clearly the rule is neater without these words, but since they do in fact seem to include prothesis, there seems no way of avoiding the complexity. In our final formulation we will collapse these two sections again into one rule in order to gain generality.

6.6.5 The last tendency of 6.6.0 takes care of the residue left by the rules just given and will have to deal with three different types of entities: [hR] [R] [əR]. There is no ordering inevitably to be assumed for these developments, save that the rule involving [əR] must follow the development of a prothetic vowel before /r/- and /u/- in those environments not handled by rule 5). Since it is simplest, however, we may begin with [hR], though we shall eventually list it last. It is clear enough that /hw/- and /hy/- lost their semivocalic component and merged with /h/-, while the resonants do not lose the resonant component, though later on /hl hm hn/ merge with /l m n/. This state of affairs can be displayed in a set of three rules:

6) a) $\begin{bmatrix} y \\ w \end{bmatrix}$ > $\emptyset$ / /h/__

    b) /hr/   >   [hr]

    c) /h/   > $\emptyset$ /__$\begin{bmatrix} l \\ m \\ n \end{bmatrix}$

Framing the rules in this way allows us to place the application of 6c) as late as we wish, and makes it possible to accommodate the facts of Homeric scansion (Chantraine 1948:175-178) as well as certain dialectal spellings with /h/ (Lejeune 1955:101). 6b) merely states that what had been a significant contrast earlier now disappears and that henceforward all initial /r/ are (redundantly) aspirated: [h] is no longer significant before resonants. We can omit 6b) in the final formulation.

6.6.6 Things are really quite simple and straightforward with the voiced sounds also. All initial voiced resonants remained as such (7c) save for /r/ and /y/, the former developing prothesis, the latter eventually merging with the product of */dy/-. At the same time we pick up initial /u/- which now develops a prothetic vowel. The only difficulty with */y/- is that *yewya by rules 1-5 should enter rule 7) as *əyewya, and *yewgos should appear as *əyewgos. Hence we must include also *əy- in our rule 7b). This fact suggests that /y/- and [əy]- first merged in */gy/- and that subsequently */gy/- was palatalized to */dy/. Hence the rules will read:

$$
7) \quad \text{a)} \quad \begin{bmatrix} u \\ r \end{bmatrix} > \begin{bmatrix} əu \\ ər \end{bmatrix}
$$

$$
\text{b)} \quad (ə)y > (/gy/) > /dy/
$$

$$
\text{c)} \quad [R] > [R]
$$

Later of course /w/ > Ø and /dy/ > ζ, but these developments can everywhere have been considerably later and in some areas must have been. /l m n/ remain unchanged by this rule, and we can therefore omit them in the final formulation.

6.6.7 This rule will affect only [əR] and is most difficult to formulate, for there is a wide variety among the low vowels in the outcome of this group of sounds, and analogical influences may well have been at work. But we have noted a few regularities in passing and can perhaps pick up a few more. Though no mention was made of the fact at the time, the prothetic vowel before /r/ is always /e/ (6.2) as it is also before /ur/- (6.4.1). We have supposed that in the majority of cases (save when an /i/ is involved) */əw/- > /aw/-, though here there are many difficulties. Furthermore we have seen (2.4.13, n. 14, al.) that /o/- tends to appear before /Rei/-. Still another observation is in order: the vowel tends to be /e/ before */Reu/- (cf. ἐλεύθερος — 2.1.6, ἐννέα — 2.3.6, Ἐλευσίς — 3.1.8), and this fact combined with the fact that /Rei/- > */oRei/- tends to suggest that some sort of dissimilation is at work. We are the more encouraged to believe that this is the case when we note that /a/- occurs only

before /ReR/- save in ἀμαλδύνω and *ἀμάργνυμι, while /e/-
appears before /a/ in ἐλαχύς and ἐλαφρός. The exceptions to be
accounted for, then, are cases in which /a/ appears before
*/Rei/- and */Reu/-, and those in which /e/- appears in posi-
tions other than before */Reu/-. /a/- appears before */Rei/- only
when */Rei/- alternates with */Roi/-, and we may therefore
assume that */ǝRei/ > */oRei/, but that */ǝRe/oi/- >
*/aRe/oi/-. This formulation at one blow removes ἀλείτης (2.1.1),
ἀλείφω (2.1.2), ἀμείβω (2.2.1), ἀείδω (3.4.2) from the class of
exceptions, but leaves ἀμεύομαι (3.2.8) unexplained, a state in
which it will have to remain: perhaps connection with ἀμείβω
ἀμοιβός is sufficient to explain the /a/. /e/- occurs in ἐνεγκεῖν
(3.3.3) and ἐλέγχω (3.1.7), thus suggesting that this is the regular
development before */RenC/-, though ἄεισι (4.4.3) here causes
difficulties. It also occurs in εἴκοσι (2.4.2) and εἴσομαι (5.3.8), and
we are thus encouraged to assume that it is regular also before
/wiy/-, even though such an assumption causes some trouble with
the o-color rule.[57] ἔνερθεν (2.3.3) instead of *ἄνερθεν remains an
exception. Given these facts and considerations, we state the

---

[57] Given these rules concerning */s/ > */h/ and dissimilation of
aspiration, we may be able to connect ἀίω (4.4.4) and οἴομαι (4.4.5) with the
root *wid- 'see, perceive, know'. All we need do is have a rule a) precede the
rules I have given:

    a) Dental > /s/ /__dental

If we do, clearly this */s/ will disappear by rule 2) if placed between vowels,
and forms with hiatus will remain. Hence οἴω would develop in the following
manner:

    a) *weid- > *weis-/__dental (in *weidʰēn?)
    2) *weis- > *weih-/__V (with /s/ introduced from *weid + dental)
    5) *weih- > *ǝweih- > οἴω
      *weisthēn > *ǝweistʰēn > οἴσθην

If we assume a second aorist *ǝwihon with the prothetic vowel brought over
from tenses in which it developed regularly, we can account also for ἄιον, as
well of course as αἰσθάνομαι. Granted that this all requires piling hypothesis
upon hypothesis, it nonetheless will work and does account for the otherwise
striking fact that words meaning 'see, know, think, perceive' in Grk. share the
elements /w/ and /i/ (plus dental).

following rule which will account for the majority of cases:

$$8) \quad /ə/ \quad > \quad /e/ \; / \_\_ \begin{bmatrix} \text{wiy} \\ \text{(u)RV} \\ \text{la} \\ \text{Re}\begin{bmatrix} u \\ n \end{bmatrix} \end{bmatrix}$$

/o/ /__Rei where /e/ does
not alternate with /o/

/a/ elsewhere

6.6.8 It remains only to give the rules in their final form.[58]

1) a) $\quad$ [R] $\quad > \quad$ [R̥]/__$\begin{bmatrix} e \\ i \end{bmatrix}$Voiceless

b) $\quad$ /lmnr/ $\quad > \quad$ [R̥]/__$\begin{bmatrix} o \\ u \end{bmatrix}$([r̥]=[w̥r̥])

b′) $\quad$ /r/ $\quad > \quad$ [R̥]/__/a/

c) $\quad$ /u/ $\quad > \quad$ [u]/__$\begin{bmatrix} r \\ l \end{bmatrix}$Vowel

$\quad\quad\quad\quad\quad\quad\quad\quad\quad\quad$ [u̥]/ elsewhere ([u̥]=[y̥u])

d) $\quad$ /w/ $\quad > \quad$ [R̥]/__$\begin{bmatrix} r \\ l \end{bmatrix}$Vowel

---

[58] In passing we might hypothesize, in spite of many difficulties, that εἴσομαι (or rather ἐίσομαι or ἐείσομαι) is an error of the aoidic tradition committed when, for whatever reason, prothesis disappeared from this form in prose, and the poets found themselves short a mora, a deficiency which they made up in the usual way by extending the initial vowel so as to fill the previous mora (above, n. 32). If this should be the case, we might, in accordance with the tendency just noted, suppose that the missing mora once was of *o*-color. If it was, then *oweisomai* would have passed to οἴσομαι, and we suddenly find ourselves with an etymological connection for οἴσω, the future of 'bring'. Semantic parallels for such a development are not far to seek: cf. ἐλευσιῶ· οἴσω (Hsch.) and modern Grk. πάω 'go' (intransitive) 'take, carry' (transitive).

e) $/y/$ > $[\mathring{R}]/\underline{\quad}\begin{bmatrix}/e\ a\ o/ \\ /us/\end{bmatrix}$

2) $/s/$ > $[h]/\begin{bmatrix}V \\ R \\ \#\end{bmatrix}\underline{\quad}\begin{bmatrix}V \\ R\end{bmatrix}$

3) $[\mathring{R}]$ > $[hR]$

4) $[hR]$ > $[R]/\underline{\quad}\begin{bmatrix}a \\ e \\ i\end{bmatrix}$ Aspirate

5) a) $[R]$ > $[\partial R]/\underline{\quad}\begin{bmatrix}RC \\ Asp\begin{bmatrix}y \\ l \\ r\end{bmatrix}\end{bmatrix}$

   b) $/r/$ > $[\partial r]/\underline{\quad}\begin{bmatrix}voiced \\ Aspirate\end{bmatrix}$

   c) $/u/$ > $[\partial u]$

   d) $[(\partial)y]$ > $(/gy/) > /dy/$

6) $/\partial/$ > $/e/ /\underline{\quad}\begin{bmatrix}wiy \\ (u)RV \\ la\begin{bmatrix}u \\ \end{bmatrix} \\ Re\begin{bmatrix}n\end{bmatrix}\end{bmatrix}$

   $/o/ /\underline{\quad}[Rei]$ where $/e/$ does not
   alternate with $/o/$

   $/a/$ elsewhere

7) $\begin{bmatrix}y \\ w\end{bmatrix}$ > $\emptyset /h/\underline{\quad}$

   $/h/$ > $\emptyset \underline{\quad}\begin{bmatrix}l \\ m \\ n\end{bmatrix}$

These rules are complicated enough in detail, but one will note that in fact they represent merely two major tendencies: aspiration of resonants and the loss of /s/ (rules 1-4), and developments involving initial resonants affected or not by rules 1-4 (rules 5-8).[59]

6.6.9 Prothesis, then, is a perfectly regular linguistic tendency in the Greek language resulting from the equally regular tendency to devoice initial (and probably other) resonants in certain environments. It is thus neither random nor haphazard, and as a result constitutes in no way a threat to the hypothesis that sound change is regular and that the rules governing it can ordinarily be stated in phonological terms. Why it is that the Greeks devoiced initial resonants in certain environments I do not know; nor do I know why initial */s/- disappeared before vowels, though I suppose it had something to do with the adoption of an IE language by speakers who had previously utilized a different linguistic system. But I do know that among the consequences of this change in articulatory habits was the development of a prothetic vowel.

---

[59] At this point a phonetic accounting for the above developments should appear. Unfortunately I cannot provide one; nor can I point to parallel developments in other languages. But one correlation of some importance does seem to emerge: prothesis occurs only before palatalizing vowels. Those vowels (/o/ and /u/) which have a component of lip-rounding do not allow prothesis, though they do favor aspiration. This fact suggests an opposition palatal-nonpalatal in the resonant system, an opposition which preceded rule 1). Subsequently some of those palatalized vowels became aspirated along with the rounded vowels, while those in a syllable closed by a resonant remained voiced and later developed prothesis. There is no doubt that palatalization in numerous ways affected the Greek consonantal system (Lejeune 1955:146-147), and indeed specifically the resonants. Furthermore Kiparsky (1967:620-621) has supposed that internal [Ry] at least passed to [Rh] (I should prefer to write [Rhy]). Hence there is evidence, though not of the most powerful sort, that both palatalization and aspiration of resonants are facts, probably related facts, of early Greek phonology, whether or not parallels can be found elsewhere.

INDEX

This book was set in type by computer photocomposition using an RCA Videocomp, model 840, at the plant of the Los Angeles Times, Inc. All of the programming for this undertaking was done by Professor David W. Packard of the University of California at Los Angeles who supervised all the stages in the preparation of the reproduction copy for photolithographing.

The roman font is based on Times Roman 11 point, and the Greek font is based on Porson Greek.

The programs and fonts were developed with the aid of a grant from the American Philological Association and with University of California research funds. The project was also assisted by Sedgwick Printout Systems of New York City. Some preliminary work was carried out at the Summer Institute in Computer Applications to Classical Studies, sponsored by the American Philological Association at the University of Illinois in Urbana in 1969, which was supported by the National Endowment for the Humanities and the Ford Foundation.